The Complete Guide to

ROOM ADDITIONS

- **Designing & Building**
- **Garage Conversions**
- **Attic Add-ons**
- **Bath & Kitchen Expansions**
- **Bump-out Additions**

D1571878

by Chris Peterson

Creative Publishing
international

MINNEAPOLIS, MINNESOTA
www.creativepub.com

Creative Publishing international

Copyright © 2011
Creative Publishing international, Inc.
400 First Avenue North, Suite 300
Minneapolis, Minnesota 55401
1-800-328-0590
www.creativepub.com

Printed in China

10 9 8 7 6 5 4 3 2 1

Library of Congress Cataloging-in-Publication Data

The complete guide to room additions : designing & building garage conversions, attic add-ons, bath & kitchen expansions, bump-out additions.
      p. cm.
  "Black & Decker."
  Includes index.
  Summary: "Provides full-color how-to information on adding livable square footage to a home, from garage conversions to bump-out expansions and dormer addditions"--Provided by publisher.
  ISBN-13: 978-1-58923-482-6 (soft cover)
  ISBN-10: 1-58923-482-0 (soft cover)
  1. Buildings--Additions. 2. Dwellings--Remodeling. I. Black & Decker Corporation (Towson, Md.) II. Title: Black & Decker complete guide to room additions.

TH4816.2.C66 2010
643'.7--dc22

2010030611

The Complete Guide to Room Additions
Created by: The Editors of Creative Publishing international, Inc., in cooperation with Black & Decker.
Black & Decker® is a trademark of The Black & Decker Corporation and is used under license.

President/CEO: Ken Fund

Home Improvement Group

Publisher: Bryan Trandem
Managing Editor: Tracy Stanley
Senior Editor: Mark Johanson

Creative Director: Michele Lanci-Altomare
Art Direction/Design: Brad Springer, Kim Winscher, James Kegley

Lead Photographer: Joel Schnell
Set Builder: James Parmeter
Production Managers: Laura Hokkanen, Linda Halls

Page Layout Artist: Danielle Smith
Tech Editor: Eric Smith
Shop Help: Charles Boldt
Proofreader: Drew Siqveland
Illustrator: Greg Maxson
Author: Chris Peterson

Cover photo: Henry Wilson/Photolibrary

NOTICE TO READERS

For safety, use caution, care, and good judgment when following the procedures described in this book. The publisher and Black & Decker cannot assume responsibility for any damage to property or injury to persons as a result of misuse of the information provided.

The techniques shown in this book are general techniques for various applications. In some instances, additional techniques not shown in this book may be required. Always follow manufacturers' instructions included with products, since deviating from the directions may void warranties. The projects in this book vary widely as to skill levels required: some may not be appropriate for all do-it-yourselfers, and some may require professional help.

Consult your local building department for information on building permits, codes, and other laws as they apply to your project.

Contents

The Complete Guide to
Room Additions

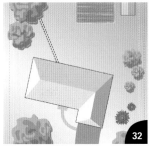

Contents (Cont.)

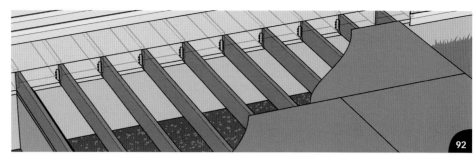

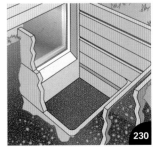

Introduction

Adding on to your home is a practical way to expand your living space with far less turmoil or expense than moving to a new house. It also provides the chance to customize your home to suit your own tastes, needs, and dreams.

Are you looking for a stylish, sun-filled home office that's positioned away from noisy traffic in the main part of the house? Have you fantasized about converting your unused attic into livable space by adding a couple of dormers and a skylight to flood the room with sunshine? Or do you dream of having a fully outfitted home theater where you could watch your favorite films in high style?

Perhaps your goals are a little more pragmatic than home theaters: you may covet a kitchen bump-out that adds crucial square footage to the most-used room in most homes. How about adding a full bathroom to create a master bedroom suite? Whatever remodeling dreams fill your head, you can bring them to life by adding on, up, out, or simply into unused space. The potential is limited only by the boundaries of your home, your property, and your imagination.

Adding or converting space gives you the chance to improve your home's overall design and general layout. You can brighten a dark interior by adding a family room with a facade of south-facing picture windows. Or, build a garage conversion with an elegant bow window to take full advantage of a lovely, secluded garden view hidden from inside the main house. Home additions can even increase curb appeal. A well-designed second-story addition with dormers and step-out terraces adds drama and interest to otherwise bland achitecture.

Achieving the room of your dreams isn't the only reason to consider building an addition. In some cases, an addition can increase your home's value—especially if that addition includes a bathroom or kitchen. If adding value is your only goal, however, you'd likely have better results investing your money elsewhere. A far more compelling reason for building an addition is that it's a way of making more of the home you already love. Add a room instead of moving and you don't have to leave cherished neighbors and friends, or pull your children out of schools you trust and know. That's the real beauty of a home addition: you get a new home just by reinventing what's already there. And in the bargain, you get to keep the neighborhood, people, and location that are so much a part of what we call home.

Gallery of Beautiful Additions

A successful room addition makes a big impact on everyone who lives in the house by altering the living space and changing the dynamics of the structure inside and out. But the most successful additions are largely invisible, blending seamlessly with the existing space and architecture so that a new visitor to the home probably wouldn't be able to detect the old from the new.

The additions shown in the following pages feature an amazing variety of possibilities: simple bump-outs that add a little space and light; an all-new living room; an elaborate attic conversion into a master suite; and many more rooms for general use or very specific functions. These examples clearly show that—whether small or large—successful additions "fit". They fit in with the home's layout and they fit with the architecture. An addition must never make the building look clunky or out of proportion, and it must never be an impediment to the interior flow of traffic, light and air.

Use the gallery of projects presented here as idea guides for designing and building a room addition that suits your home and life. Or simply view them as inspiration, providing you with some idea of the breadth and scope available for growing your space and changing your home to the place you always dreamed it would be.

A brand-new, window-filled wing nearly doubled the interior living space in this house. Plus, the new L-shaped footprint allowed the homeowners to convert their plain patio into an intimate courtyard.

Case Study No. 1

Adding an entire new wing to your home is a major project and the cost can easily equal or eclipse the current value of your house. But in the end you'll find it's almost like gaining a second house, so the investment is usually worthwhile. In the addition featured on these two pages (see page 8 also for a bigger view), the new living space afforded by the added wing allowed for a major expansion to the kitchen and dining area within the original part of the house.

VIEW INTO ADDITION FROM KITCHEN IN ORIGINAL HOUSE

A sunny room is a welcome feature in any home. Located right at the corner of the ell formed by the addition and the original house, this full-lite entry door system lets warmth and sunshine into both the old house and the new.

VIEW FROM INSIDE ADDITION TOWARD KITCHEN

The consistent window style between the old section and the new section of the expanded house is the visual glue that ties all of the elements together. Windows with distinctive styling, such as these multi-lite Colonial style double-hungs, are especially good for this task. Here, the effect is further enhanced by adding entry doors and even cabinet doors that share the same basic style and appearance.

VIEW TOWARD ADDITION FROM DINING ROOM

The expanded dining area in the original house has sightlines to both the interior and the exterior of the new wing addition.

Case Study No. 2

BEFORE

AFTER

A relatively large bumpout addition with a hip roof is tied into the original house structure and roof line, adding plenty of new space and also creating an intimate spot for a deck and dining area with some shelter and privacy. The new square footage takes the place of an overhead shade structure that was enclosed with beaded siding panels and contributed little to the appearance of the house.

VIEW OF KITCHEN EXPANSION FROM ADDITION AREA

Expanding the original kitchen into part of the addition created enough new floorspace that a sizable kitchen island could be added to the prep area. New flooring throughout integrates the new and old areas.

VIEW TOWARD STREET FROM INSIDE ADDITION

An unobstructed wide angle view of the yard and streetscape, as seen from inside the completed addition. The knotty pine beaded ceiling gives a bit of northwoods flavor to the new living space in this Minnesota home.

Case Study No. 3

AFTER

A second-story addition maintains the natural lines and style of this two-story home, but adds abundant indoor and outdoor space. A successful addition is nearly impossible to detect and this one is so fluid that only by looking at the home as it was before the change is it clear where the structure was modified. Note that the second story window in the "Before" photo was saved and reinstalled with flanking windows in the add-on.

BEFORE

**VIEW THROUGH WINDOW
BANK ON UPPER LEVEL**

A bright, restful seating area is added to a plain bedroom thanks to the addition. The built-in window seats at the ends of the expansion make the room feel as if it were original to the house.

VIEW OF FRONT PORCH

Room additions create new exterior opportunities in almost every case. In fact, with some careful planning the new exterior details can outshine the interior expansion. The spacious open porch on this house, with its rich wood ceiling, adds outdoor livability and a new patio-door entry to this house.

Case Study No. 4

Additions to houses on tight lots require some creativity, but every little bit of new space will be appreciated. This cottage-style house was built on a lot with virtually no room for side to side expansion, but a small front yard offered some possibilities for growing the footprint without turning the house into a box shape. The small, single story bumpout went a long way toward making the interior feel spacious and open.

OPPOSITE PAGE, TOP. Although this bumpout addition created just enough new space to accommodate an entryway and one new sofa in the living room, it was just enough to let the other rooms relax. Instead of looking like a tiny closet tucked in the corner, the kitchen became a more prominent feature simply by virtue of having its own wall.

OPPOSITE PAGE, BOTTOM. Standing in the new doorway you truly understand why this style of house is often referred to as a "Shotgun." Lengthening the house with the front addition enhances the narrowness and adds to the shotgun effect that many find desirable.

VIEW LOOKING OUT THROUGH ADDITION

VIEW STANDING IN DOORWAY OF ADDITION

Case Study No. 5

Where does it say that an addition must be styled exactly like the rest of your house? Sometimes, a wildly contrasting style can be very successful. This bumpout addition is designed in a modernist cube form, which shares virtually no architectural feature with the ranch house to which it is attached. A purist might describe the effect as "remuddling," but for the homeowner it's more a case of having the best of both worlds.

**VIEW LOOKING INTO
ADDITION AT NIGHT**

A cloak of darkness minimizes the contrasting architectural styles while reinforcing the notion that large windows can be as much about looking in as they are about looking out.

VIEW LOOKING OUT THROUGH LARGE PICTURE WINDOW

One of the many advantages of the altered space is increased exposure to the backyard view and light. This picture window was purposely planned to frame the group of trees.

VIEW LOOKING INTO KITCHEN WORK AREA

The side of the addition uses clerestory windows to bring in light, while attractive wood cabinets block an unimpressive side-yard view. Thoughtful design features like this help make a new space more livable and inviting.

Case Study No. 6

ELEVATION VIEW OF COMPLETED TWO-STORY BUMPOUT

This two-story room addition is about outdoor spaces as well as indoor spaces. While the new children's bedroom, Jack & Jill bathroom, and family room were the driving reasons for the addition, the covered patio, balcony and spa terrace proved to be the real gems created by the project.

SIDE VIEW OF COMPLETED TWO-STORY BUMP-OUT

From the side or from the rear, this carefully planned and meticulously executed room addition meets one of the key tests many designers would put to it: Does it look like it has always been there?

INTERIOR VIEW OF COMPLETED TWO-STORY BUMPOUT

A pair of windows in the remodeled master bathroom looks out toward the spa area. The master bath repeats the dark wood tones and buff wall colors featured on the exterior of the house and addition.

Case Study No. 7

SIDE VIEW OF COMPLETED WING ADDITION

Filled with light-gathering windows, this addition visually opens up an older brick home, modernizing without corrupting the existing historic architecture. The distinctive steel roof effectively unifies the two structures despite different siding styles.

FRONT VIEW OF COMPLETED WING ADDITION

The glass-fronted facade of the addition comes to life at night with a cheery, welcoming glow. The planning stage of any addition should consider all aspects, all exposures at all times.

INTERIOR VIEW NO. 1 OF WING ADDITION

One of the advantages of an addition is that it allows you to incorporate small luxuries you've dreamed about over time, like the light-soaked window seat shown here.

INTERIOR VIEW NO. 2 OF WING ADDITION

This addition's abundant windows not only let light in, they also exploit the spectacular views surrounding this secluded home. Window placement is key to effectively planning a successful addition.

Case Study No. 8

EXTERIOR VIEW OF OCTAGONAL ROOM ADDITION

Based on an octagonal form that is more typical to gazebo design than addition design, this spacious new room creates a retreat from the fairly nondescript exterior of this house. At first glance, you might assume that the enclosed space is a three-season or four-season porch. But the lavish trimwork details, such as the frame-and-panel wainscoting, quickly inform you that this is indeed fully-developed living space with a formal attitude.

INTERIOR VIEW OF OCTAGONAL ROOM ADDITION

Case Study No. 9

EXTERIOR VIEW OF DORMER ADDITIONS

A gambrel-style (roughly) dormer built over a new portico offers both interior and exterior benefits. The smaller dormer further up the roof converts a kneewall area into a cozy seating spot.

INTERIOR VIEW OF SMALLER DORMER

The inviting window seat and the fancy arched window are made possible by a simple dormer expansion that's cut into the roofline of this two-dormer project. Beadboard wainscoting extends into the rear area of the dormer to help it blend into the room.

Additional Addition Ideas

**LARGE DORMER
EXPANSION
OVER GARAGE**

This second-story bumpout over a double garage adds two new bedrooms and plenty of extra curb appeal to this formerly plain, small house. Be aware that when you add living space over garages you almost always need to make modifications to the garage ceiling to conform to fire prevention aspects of building codes.

**TWO-STORY
VAULTED GREATROOM**

The sky is the limit when planning an addition, as this two-story, one-room expansion confirms. The vaulted ceiling allows for stunning tall windows that give loft and light to this house.

GLASS-WALL SUNPORCH OFF KITCHEN

Continuing the clay-tile roofline downward to cover this bumpout integrates the room with the house despite the obvious differences of the all-glass walls. The sizable hole in the exterior wall created to make the addition is fitted with an accordion-style track door that can be drawn closed for privacy or during cold spells.

CATHEDRAL CEILING FAMILY ROOM

Attached to the one end of a large suburban home, this addition creates a beautiful, airy space for family relaxation time. A beautiful wood beam at the top of the vaulted cathedral ceiling creates a lovely contrast with the two-story fieldstone fireplace built into the gabled glass wall.

(continued)

ROOM-SIZED DORMER OVER ENTRYWAY

The gable profiles from the ends of a plain hip roof are repeated in this large dormer expansion. By cutting into the house a couple of feet below the eave line, the designers were able to provide a full-height, 8 ft-ceiling in the new room without raising the roof. The solution is a bit unorthodox, but it succeeds here because the homeowners were willing to sacrifice some ceiling height in the foyer area just inside the entry door.

CALIFORNIA SUNROOM EXPANSION

This two-story, soft-contemporary house in suburban California was a fine single-family home with three upstairs bedrooms, but the owners wanted a little more living space on the main floor. Luckily, they had some room to grow. They added this large library/sunroom addition to take some of the pressure off of the other common areas. By siding it with a manufactured stone veneer instead of more stucco they kept their home from crossing visually into the monster mansion category and gave the addition its own identity.

ADD A SECOND STORY TO A RAMBLER

Ramblers and bungalows were popular American home styles built in the second half of the 20th Century. But their one-story floorplans present livability issues as families grow. By adding a second story with two bedrooms centered over the home entry, this fairly plain rambler takes on the look and feel of a historic Colonial house, complete with shutters, windows and architectural columns that appear in both the old and the new sections.

A CLASSIC ATTIC CONVERSION

An addition or conversion is mostly about creating new living space. In this well-executed conversion of an unfinished attic, a single long, narrow lofted area brings a host of new options to the house, including a home office or a family room. The exposed rafters were clad in rustic, rough-sawn lumber to imitate the look of timber post-and-beam framing. Three new windows on the west wall introduce plenty of natural light.

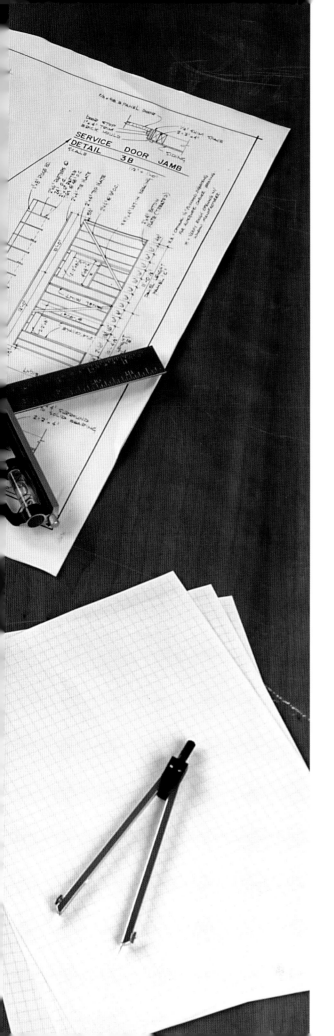

Planning
& Design

Every home addition starts with a dream. No matter what your own dream is, making an actual addition match is always the result of careful planning and thoughtful design.

The planning process begins with a thorough evaluation of what's already there. Inspect your home and property for a better understanding of how the home was built, and uncover potential problems. Once you've finished, you can begin the enjoyable exercise of designing your new space. This usually involves sketching out the addition and selecting the elements that will give it character. Windows, doors, siding, and roofing establish the visual continuity between the house and the addition. Sketching them to scale will give you a feel for how well the addition will integrate. These initial sketches form the basis for the highly detailed drafted plans that will guide the actual construction.

Early in the process you'll need to decide how much of the work you want to do yourself. In addition to the actual construction work, you may need professionals to help you work out the fine points of your building plan, start the permit application process, craft a budget, and establish a realistic schedule. Plan well, and you'll spare yourself a lot of headaches along the way.

In this chapter:

- Evaluating Your House
- Integrating the Addition
- Your Budget & Financing
- Codes and Etiquette
- Drawing Plans
- Project Scheduling
- The Green Addition

Evaluating Your House

A thorough evaluation of the existing structure is the first step in determining if an addition can be supported by the load-bearing parts of the house and the mechanical systems that are already in place. The evaluation will help you determine what, if any, upgrades will be necessary. A basic inspection also gives you the chance to detect and address problems that might hold up construction, such as a termite infestation or a buckling foundation. You can also take this opportunity to identify and address problems of a more general nature, such as an aging roof or inadequate drainage.

Start your evaluation at the bottom of the house and work upward systematically, keeping a written record of all your observations. Take your time to be objective—you can't wish your house into better condition.

Begin your home evaluation with the foundation walls, visually inspecting the inside surfaces. Look for cracks, bulging and bowing, and any signs of water damage or pest infestation.

The Foundation

Inspect your foundation from the inside first; you may be able to see cracks or buckling that is hidden below grade on the outside. Cracks are usually caused by settling or movement of the house or soil. It's wise to fix any you find because they are potential avenues for water infiltration and a gateway for bugs and pests. The best way to repair a concrete wall crack is to inject a special epoxy that creates an expandable, flexible seal. If you have several radiating cracks, or cracks larger than ¼ inch to ½ inch, you should consult a professional to determine the underlying cause. Cracks in concrete block usually follow the mortar lines and if they are more than hairline cracks the blocks should be repointed.

Foundation Wall Warning Signs

Bulging foundation walls are a more serious issue than a few cracks and usually call for professional expertise and some knowledge of structural engineering. This problem must be remedied before any other walls are added to the foundation. The solution usually entails adding vertical support beams or a buttress wall or, in more severe cases, the buckled wall may need to be entirely rebuilt.

Leaks are a common problem and point to poor drainage on the outside of the foundation. In many cases, you can improve the foundation drainage during the process of expanding the foundation for a room addition. You should repair any leaks you discover, even if it does not directly affect the addition.

Inspect for pests, especially if there is evidence of water damage. Termites build tubes that can be found on walls or along wood beams or joists, while other wood boring insects leave piles of wood shavings and droppings. If you find signs of insect damage or infestation, you need to exterminate as soon as possible and certainly before construction of the new space begins. If the infestation is severe, consider hiring a professional to test the wood and determine if structural members have been compromised. Of course, you also need to remedy any underlying moisture and crack problems that drew the insects in the first place.

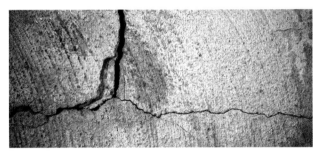

Large cracks in concrete foundation walls indicate settling. Contact a structural engineer.

Exposed reinforcement indicates major concrete deterioration. Consult a licensed contractor.

Structural modifications and major repairs often weaken a wall and should be checked by an engineer.

Moisture infiltration is easy to identify by white efflorescence and even growth of plant roots and mold.

Mold often reveals itself in failed paint, indicating a water problem that needs addressing.

Insects, rodents, snakes, and other pests can get into very small openings and are usually detected by direct observation.

Exterior Inspection Points

Next, inspect the outside of the house. Check plumb and level of walls and the foundation where a room addition will attach to the main house. Although it's common for houses to settle slightly out of plumb over time, it's important to be aware of variations so that you can adjust the new construction. Check siding for signs of wear or damage such as water infiltration, missing or cracked sections, or missing corner caps. Inspect the mortar joints of brick walls and the seams of vinyl or aluminum siding. Scrutinize wood shingles or lap siding for signs of mold or rot.

Examine exterior windows and doors as part of your survey. Any addition increases the workload of the home's heating and cooling systems, so you want to ensure the house is as weathertight as possible. If the windows are old, single-pane units, the addition may be just the excuse you need to upgrade to more energy-efficient windows all around. Verify that weatherstripping is intact around doors and windows, and that the casing joints are properly flashed, caulked, and watertight.

Gutters and downspouts should be in good condition to prevent future water damage and leaks.

Make sure the gutters slope ¼ inch for every 8 feet to 10 feet of run. Also check that the flashing is intact along roof valleys and around chimneys, skylights, vents, and other features projecting up through the roof. While you're on the roof, inspect it for signs of damage or age deterioration, such as cupping or cracked shingles. If the addition involves altering the roof—such as building a dormer—it's essential to make sure the existing roof is in good condition.

Rotted and damaged basement windows don't necessarily indicate a problem—they simply need to be replaced from time to time.

Siding damage in and of itself isn't a problem, but check to make sure no water has infiltrated through the damage and into the wall.

Damage from pests, including birds, flying insects, squirrels, and bats should be repaired immediately. Inspect around the damage to make sure pests haven't infiltrated beyond the entry points.

Rotted fascia almost always indicates a roof leak that is allowing water to run behind the fascia boards.

Gutters and downspouts should be leak-free and in good general condition.

Radon ▸

Test for excessive radon. Radon is an odorless, colorless, radioactive gas that can enter through basement floors and accumulate, posing a health hazard. Some smoke detectors will detect radon, but only if it is already at dangerous levels. To determine if you have a potential radon problem, you can purchase a fairly expensive digital radon detector, or you can buy an inexpensive home detection kit available at hardware stores. You simply take an air sample with the kit collector and mail the sample to the laboratory. In most cases, you'll receive a report with recommendations in a week or two.

The Professional Home Inspection ▸

A certified professional home inspector can be a worthwhile expense if you're considering an extensive addition and have lived in the house for a long time. The inspector will provide a fresh pair of eyes that might catch problems you've lived with for so long that you no longer notice them.

The inspector will also bring a working familiarity with best standards and practices for all the mechanical systems in the house. You can expect your inspector to give you a realistic, objective assessment of any potential problems or existing areas of concern—especially as they relate to adding space onto or into the structure.

Look for an inspector certified with the American Society of Home Inspectors, and check references. Choose a local professional who will be familiar with the common construction practices, architectural history, and external conditions in your specific geographic region. Tag along on the inspection; it will give you a chance to ask questions and get explanations about any concerns the inspector raises. Inspectors are usually more than happy to explain their findings as they go along.

However, be aware that home inspectors don't advise on code requirements or assess the sales value of homes. If you have a question about whether your home meets current code requirements, you'll need to consult the local building department. But the inspector will be able to give you an informed and comprehensive picture of the current state of your home's structure and systems. Expect a written report detailing the inspector's findings. That will, in turn, give you a good idea of what you might need to fix before jumping into building your addition.

Evaluating Your Mechanical Systems

Any new home addition increases the burden on the existing heating, ventilation, and air conditioning systems, as well as the electrical service and the plumbing. When you add more square footage to your floor plan, you're also increasing the amount of air that needs to be heated and cooled, adding more load to the electrical service and, in some cases, adding to the existing plumbing. It's crucial to assess how prepared your current systems are to deal with the extra load.

Electrical. Almost every addition requires at least a base minimum of electrical outlets and lighting receptacles. The more complex the addition, the more power it will need. Depending on your current heating and cooling capacity, the addition may also need power for electric heaters and air conditioners. Given the danger involved, most homeowners choose to leave electrical work to a professional. This is wise.

When it comes to assessing electrical needs and capacity, it helps to know the basics of how electricity is distributed in the house. Overhead electrical service comes in through a service head and is routed down to your main service panel through large conductors called service entry cables. There, the service is split into many different circuits. Each circuit serves a different room or area in the house, and the circuits should be labeled in the breaker box. Depending on the amperage of the service coming into the house (these days, a 200 amp panel is usually the minimum), the box may have one or more unused circuits that you can dedicate to a new space.

If you're converting a space such as a full attic or garage, it's likely that an existing circuit already serves that space. It is unlikely, however, that your post-conversion electrical demand will be met by the existing circuit or circuits. If you're creating an entirely new space such as a room addition, it is virtually guaranteed that you'll need to run at least one new circuit, if not a subpanel with several branch circuits.

When building an addition, it's not uncommon that an upgrade to your home's main service panel is needed. If your circuit breaker or fuse box is full or you have 100 amp service, consult a professional.

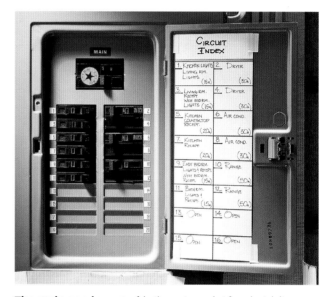

The main service panel is the entry point for electricity coming into your home. If your panel does not have enough open slots or sufficient capacity to power a new addition, you'll need to hire an electrician to upgrade your service. In most cases it's best to take care of the upgrade before you break ground.

Circuit Capacity ▸

Use this form to do a quick calculation of circuit capacity. Compare the result of your calculations to the average dedicated circuit that supplies 20 amps at 120 volts providing a total capacity of 2,400 watts (which translates to a usable capacity of about 1,900 watts).

If the total exceeds the capacity of the circuit servicing the addition, you'll need to plan for another circuit or run appliances or receptacles on other circuits with available capacity.

ELECTRIC CIRCUIT CAPACITY EVALUATION

Item	Use	Total
Addition sq. ft.	× 3 watts =	_____
# of small appliances	× 1500 watts =	_____
# of large appliances	× (wattages = on nameplates)	_____
Electrical heater/room AC	× sized to = suit sq. ftg.	_____

HVAC. Your heating, ventilation, and cooling system (HVAC) was most likely sized to efficiently serve your home's current square footage. Adding a room addition of 200 square feet or more impacts how hard your furnace and central air conditioning have to work. How much it stresses the system depends on the location of the space. It's a good idea to hire a heating and cooling professional to advise you on the best option for integrating your new space with the current system. Bear in mind that sometimes the best alternative for the mechanicals is a localized solution, such as baseboard heating and a window air conditioner. Even if your HVAC system has enough capacity to service the new space, connecting a new space to a central heating and cooling system is going to mean running new ductwork for a forced air system, or pipes for a hot water system. It may be easier to use local solutions.

Plumbing. If your addition will include a bathroom, kitchen, wet bar, or other water-consuming function, you'll need to determine if your water heater and water supply lines are beefy enough to deliver the water you need. New supply lines may negatively impact the water pressure in the house to the point that you need to increase the size of the water supply lines. Waste lines and vents also need to be checked for capacity, so that you aren't overwhelming your waste line or septic capacity. Hot water for a new sink, and especially for a shower or bath, will make a significant impact on your hot water system. If the load doesn't change (if the number of showers and people taking them remains the same), your current hot water heater should be able to meet demand. However, if the new bathroom is going to see a lot of additional use, or if you sometimes run out of hot water now, you will need to plan for either a larger water heater or a supplemental water heater positioned near or in the new addition.

Adding new outlets and inlets to your current HVAC system is almost always the best long-term solution for additions. But there are some instances where it might make sense to opt for a more localized solution, such as a window air conditioner or an electric baseboard heater.

Roughing in new plumbing lines for a kitchen or bathroom addition is a relatively big project, but not difficult if you have DIY experience. Check codes and consult your building inspector for pipe sizes, slope, and other requirements.

Evaluating Your Site

The features of your property play almost as large a part in the planning and design process as the features of your house. Local codes and regulations controlling the size of structures, the maximum percentage of a lot that can be built upon, and the minimum setback requirements are all important determining factors in most addition plans. Along with regulations, your property's topography and exposure should influence the building site. For instance, a yard that slopes severely or has extremely irregular terrain may present challenges to building a room addition foundation. In reviewing your property you also need to check with the local utility companies to determine and mark the location of any buried utilities (call 811). It's far easier to identify these lines prior to construction than it is to repair a ruptured main.

Setback. The setback is the minimum distance that must be maintained between your structure and your property line. Setbacks are established for a number of reasons including safety and clear access to public thoroughfares. Setbacks obviously affect bump-outs and other types of additions that increase the footprint of your structure, but they can also impact garage conversions. If the rules allow for a non-dwelling structure to be close to the property line, converting it to a living space may suddenly violate the setback rules for dwellings.

Easements. You'll also need to take into account any easements on your property. All easements effectively do the same thing: they limit building on parts of your property so that those parts can be accessed by other parties. Common easements include "easements in gross" that allow power, water, and cable companies critical access to utilities on, or crossing, your property. Appurtenances are "easements in common," such as a driveway that crosses your property so that a neighbor can get to theirs. These, like many property easements you'll encounter, are obvious. Others are not. That's why you should check your deed and title for descriptions of property easements before you settle on the final location for your addition.

Code Limitations. Building codes and regulations normally limit how far up you can build, as well as how far out. A local code may allow for an attic conversion that adds dormers, but restricts a second-story addition that raises the height of exterior walls.

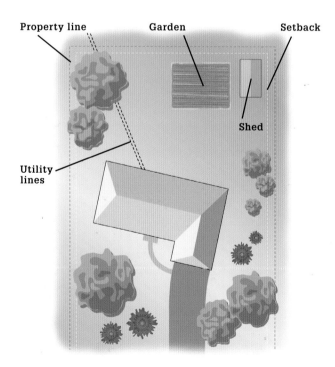

A plan view of your yard that includes all permanent structures will help you determine which codes and regulations will impact your design.

A severe slope in back of this house makes adding on a challenge requiring specialized pier-and-post foundations.

Assessing Your Soil ▸

An important part of evaluating the suitability of your property for a room addition is determining if your soil is going to present any challenges in laying the foundation. Different types of soil can actually add to construction costs because of the extra work required in excavating or reinforcing the foundation. That said, it's always easier to deal preemptively with soil issues as they occur than to fix the many and severe problems unstable soil can create.

The first place to go for information on the soil in your area is your county extension service. They'll be able to give you information about the type of soil in your region. If you don't have a local office, you can contact the United States Department of Agriculture and request a soil map for your area. The type of soil largely determines what problems may occur and what preventative steps are called for.

- **Clay:** Clay shrinks and expands during dry and wet periods more than other soils do. If you have high clay content in your soil, anticipate extra work in

laying the foundation. You'll need to spend more time and effort on the drainage system to direct water well away from the area of the foundation.

- **Sand:** Sandy soil is subject to shifting and movement, but is only a serious problem when the sand content is very high, such as along a river or in a coastal area. If you suspect your soil has an unusually high sand content, get a soil analysis. This may lead you to use a different type of foundation for the addition, such as deep piers rather than a poured concrete wall foundation.

- **Muck:** When soil contains large sections of decomposing organic matter, or "muck," the soil base can become quite unstable. If built on, the soil may compress over time, causing detrimental settling in the years to come. If you encounter a lot of muck in excavating a foundation, the most reliable solution is to excavate all of it and replace it with more stable soil. Although this may seem excessive, it's a matter of heading off far worse problems down the road.

Determining what type of soil you'll be dealing with in excavating for a foundation is crucial to planning for an addition. Common types include gravel and sandy gravel (left), sandy (middle), and clay/silt (right).

Evaluating Sun Exposure

Never underestimate the power of the sun. Using sun exposure to your advantage can ensure that your addition is warm and cool at the right times, makes the space more energy efficient, and provides natural light when and where you want it.

Planning for sun exposure means taking into account not only changes throughout the day, but also throughout the seasons. Given the variables, the first step in evaluating your sun exposure is to look at how your current structure is oriented. The basic fact that the sun rises in the east and sets in the west means that east-facing walls and windows are going to receive bright sun in the morning with shade in the afternoon. In addition, because of our position above the equator, southern exposures receive more light through the day than northern exposures do. This is why the most energy-efficient buildings are designed with their longest wall facing south—it allows the building to collect the maximum solar heat throughout the day.

The sun also provides abundant light, which is another factor in designing new or converting existing spaces. If you're building a home office in an attic in May, you might position a dormer or skylight so that natural light streams down on you as you work at your desk. But that same sun will be lower in winter, and may be right in your eyes come December. When sunlight hits the addition can be every bit as important as where; you won't welcome early morning light through the east-facing window of a bedroom quite as happily as you would in a kitchen.

Natural and man-made structures on or near your property may block or filter sunlight, another consideration in moderating the effect of sunlight. For example, you can plant a tree to shade a picture window during the hottest part of the day.

The best way to plan for all the variables is to do a "sun survey" prior to finalizing plans for the new space. Sketch out the sun's position relative to your property at regular intervals throughout the day. Make a simple map of the property and include shadings for those areas where direct light is blocked by trees or other structures. Use this simple guide when planning the location and orientation of windows, skylights, and the addition itself, and you'll put the power of the sun to work for you.

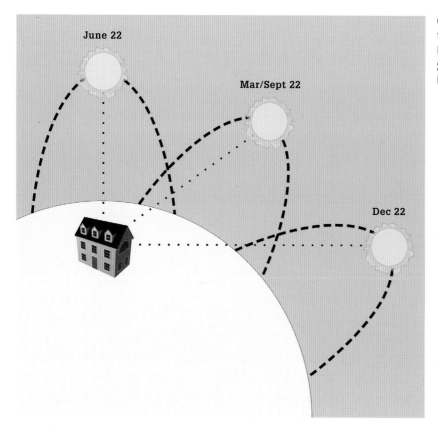

Consider the seasonal movement of the sun when designing your addition. Ideally, windows will allow passive solar gain in winter and reflect the sun's rays in summer.

From Inside Looking Out

Because it's where you'll spend most of your time, the interior of any addition is the primary area of concern in design and planning. The view from inside the new space involves both practical and aesthetic considerations. On the practical side, being a good neighbor means not positioning new windows directly in line with your neighbor's windows. This can be a matter of privacy—such as positioning an attic dormer so that it does not look directly into your neighbor's upstairs bedroom. You may also have more specific reasons for window placement; if you're adding a kitchen onto the back of the house, it might be very important for you to keep an eye on your kids playing in the backyard while you prepare meals.

Beyond these practical considerations, a nice view becomes part of the beauty of an addition. Although this may entail placing windows overlooking a garden, more likely it means changing the view to suit where the windows are to be placed. Adding a room or converting a garage may entail a bit of additional landscaping to block a view, such as your neighbor's garbage cans, or to add a pleasing vista, such as a new four-season flowerbed.

As important as the view from inside may be, the impact the addition has on the look of the property and house as a whole is substantial. Any change to the architecture alters the way viewers perceive the home. A room addition can have an especially powerful impact on your yard and garden, cutting into outdoor space as you increase interior square footage. The best addition maintains a pleasing balance between inside and out, just as it integrates fluidly with the home's exterior architecture.

Stand in the proposed building area (if you have access) and imagine the view from inside the addition looking out. Choose a site and an orientation that frames the best parts of your yard, as this bathroom window does.

Integrating the Addition

The most successful home additions don't announce themselves—they blend seamlessly with the existing home style and architecture. The trick is, in a word, continuity. The layout of the house should flow as well or better than ever once the addition is in place. The new space should merge with the existing structure through the use of architectural features, both inside and outside. The idea of achieving continuity is most essential when integrating a separate room addition, but the principle also applies in converting an existing space such as an attic or garage.

The key to maintaining—or even improving—the flow of traffic, light and air through the home is the transition between the addition and the existing structure. A wide open transition creates very natural movement from one space to another, but is appropriate only in common rooms such as a family room added onto a living area. If the addition is a bedroom or other room where privacy is of the essence, the transition will need to be a door. In this case, using a door and casing that matches those in the house will make the transition more fluid.

In the case of an attic conversion the transition is in the form of a staircase. The shape—wide or narrow, straight run, L- or U-shaped, or spiral—determines how linked into the new space the original is. Take your cues from other staircases in the house. Other elements can also help tie the spaces together, such as a roof window that funnels sunlight down to the lower floors.

Architectural features are even more powerful elements of continuity. These are indicators that create a visual flow between the new space and old. Continue the home's crown and base moldings, and picture and chair rails into the addition to tie it to the other rooms in the house. Fixtures serve the same role. For example, if you've chosen distinctive overhead light fixtures for your house, use a matching fixture in the addition to give the eye another clue that the space is part of the whole. Match the door and window casings to further reinforce visual continuity. Integrating the exterior of an addition is a matter of matching roof pitch and roofing material, siding, window and door styles, and even landscaping.

By repeating the distinctive Craftsman-style trimwork and eave treatment, this above-garage room addition blends seamlessly into the large Craftsman house to which it is attached.

A Computer-Aided Preview of Your Addition ▸

With all the considerations that go into how your addition is positioned in relation to the rest of the house and property, it's sometimes difficult to envision how it will look from all angles and perspectives, even with the help of architectural and construction drawings. That's where computer-aided design (CAD) programs can help. Originally designed as high-end architectural rendering software, many of today's CAD programs are designed specifically for the homeowner.

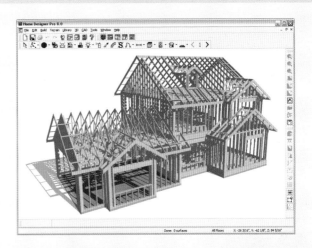

These programs usually require very little expertise. With a modicum of practice you can use the software to create a model of your current home and landscaping and then incorporate the addition to see how it will look. Some CAD programs even allow for 3-D rotation, to give you an idea of what the structure will look like as you walk around the house. Most of these type of programs have a wealth of interesting features, allowing you to digitally "frame and finish" the addition, calculate the amount of materials you'll need, and even get a sense of how the addition will look with different paint, siding, roofing and architectural ornamentation. Many programs offer the ability to produce drawings from your renderings, but not all building departments accept computer-rendered drawings.

Still, these programs represent the chance to preview, in a very realistic way, just what the addition will look like in place, with a minimum of time and effort.

Floor Transitions ▸

Weave new floorboards into old floorboards if you want the addition floor to look original. Otherwise, simply use a transition strip.

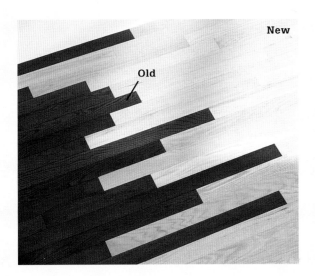

New

Old

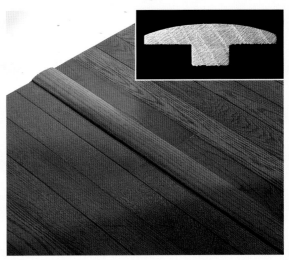

Your Budget & Financing

Even modest additions are not inexpensive. If the addition is ambitious, the cost can grow rapidly, often eclipsing the price of the house in the first place. When dealing with that level of expense, it's wise to establish an accurate budget before the work starts, and then adhere to the budget as the project proceeds.

Unless you have a serious fascination with accountancy, the budgeting process is far less exciting than actually designing your addition. But developing your budget does actually help you make critical decisions that will affect the design. You may have fallen in love with that handmade imported Italian tile, but seeing the real costs quite probably will break the spell. Assigning numbers to your dream space often brings things right down to Earth, but it can also head off worst-case scenarios—like running out of money before you finish the addition.

As daunting as the process may seem, don't fall into the trap of handing over the budget responsibilities to a contractor or other professional; the person you hire is going to be much less careful about spending your money than you are. However, don't hesitate to borrow from the expertise of numerous professionals. For example, developers and contractors often use an average per-square-foot multiplier that can help you to roughly estimate the baseline cost of an addition.

A detailed budget is not just a tool for controlling project spending; it's also required if you want to obtain financing for the project. Most homeowners will need to finance at least part of their addition. In fact, the tax incentives surrounding a home equity loan often are the driving force behind a homeowner's decision to invest in a major home addition. But even if you are paying for the addition out of pocket, you'll need a realistic cost estimate when you apply for your building permit (permit fees are usually based on actual cost estimates).

Estimating Costs ▸

Take a trip to your local home center and record the price of materials: even if a contractor insists on using their own sources for materials, the cost to you should be comparable to retail. Add in the fees for any professionals you'll use (get detailed estimates from them first). Then, add in the costs of associated services such as ordering a concrete truck and permit fees. Finally, any home addition budget should include 10 to 20 percent padding for cost overruns and the surprises that always seem to pop up with any large home improvement project.

Without thorough, realistic budgeting and planning, building an addition—even a minor one—can quickly turn into a nightmare project.

Financing Options

Obtaining financing is a critical part of most addition projects. Unless you have access to private resources like a rich uncle or a trust fund, commercial lenders are really the only option for home improvement loans. Here are the basic products you'll encounter in the financing marketplace.

- **Home equity line of credit.** This allows you access to funds as you need them, usually at a favorable interest rate. Depending on your financial circumstances, you may also be able to deduct the interest from your income taxes.
- **Second mortgage.** A second mortgage is a lump-sum loan that, like a home equity loan, leverages the equity you have in your home. You can deduct the interest on a second mortgage and if your credit is good and your home equity is substantial, you'll qualify for a competitive interest rate, similar to a new mortgage.
- **FHA loan.** The Federal Housing Authority administers a "rehabilitation" loan program that covers some addition projects (especially those that are measurably "green" or that include a general upgrade of the energy efficiency of the house). The loans come with many strings and up-front requirements, but if you meet guidelines, this can be a great low-interest financing option.
- **Credit cards and lines of credit.** These are usually the least attractive methods of financing and are best used as "bridge" financing to get the ball rolling when you anticipate receiving a large chunk of money in the near future or are waiting for a loan to close.
- **Construction loan.** The construction loan is an alternative to a home equity loan and the terms will be comparable. To oversimplify the decision a bit, if the value of the house after the addition will not exceed the first mortgage plus the construction loan, then you should probably opt for another form of financing.

Borrowing money has plenty of hidden costs like settlement fees and origination fees. Be sure to work with a financial advisor to estimate the real and complete costs of financing a home addition and read all the fine print.

Codes

Dealing with zoning regulations and building codes may not be your idea of fun, but the underlying reasons for these rules—to standardize construction within the community and establish best standards and practices to ensure the ongoing integrity of existing structures—are undeniably compelling. Codes ensure buildings are safe and they protect the resale value of homes in the community. That's why the long road of planning for a home addition inevitably and inescapably runs through local building departments and sometimes zoning boards.

Local codes are generally based on national codes such as the National Electrical Code, the Uniform Plumbing Code, and the International Residential Code. And though the reputable professionals you hire will likely be well acquainted with local codes, it's a good idea to review them yourself. For instance, some codes require that as part of any major remodeling project, systems such as electrical be upgraded to meet current code. A provision like this could add significant expense and extra work, so it's best to know how it will affect the project before you begin actual construction.

Regulations and codes also detail what type of construction plans you'll need to submit for work permits. Many localities require that plans be drafted and submitted by a certified engineer or architect.

The permit process involves fees for the initial application and a payment when the permits are issued, usually tied to the budgeted cost of the project. The process can affect scheduling. Once permits are issued, the clock begins to tick; building departments only allow a certain amount of time between issuing the permits and completion of the project—180 days is common (though they can be renewed). Make sure you know what the deadline is and keep it in mind while you're monitoring the project schedule.

Once the construction begins, it's more important than ever to ensure that the actual work maintains code compliance. If an inspector discovers a code violation, the whole project can come to a halt so that the violation can be remedied and a new inspection scheduled. Major code violations can be punished with legal actions ranging from cease-and-desist notices that stop all work on the site indefinitely, to destruction orders that require you to demolish and remove already completed construction. On top of that, you could be fined.

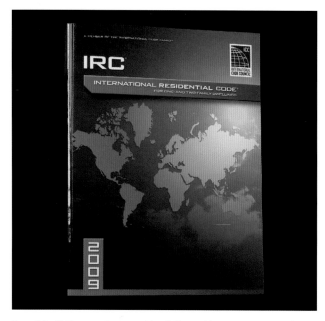
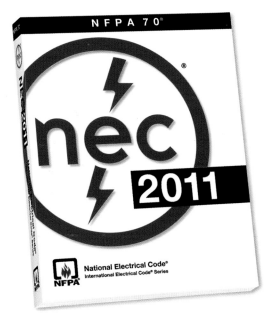

Local building codes must be followed in every aspect of your addition plan and construction process. Most codes are based on published national codes, such as the ones above. In all cases, local codes supercede national codes, however, so it is important for you to involve your municipal building department from the outset.

Be a Courteous Neighbor ▸

Local codes aren't the only regulations that will affect a home addition project. Homeowner association regulations can be even more restrictive. Where local authorities are trying to ensure safe and reasonable construction, homeowner associations are concerned with the more rigid goal of maintaining standardized aesthetics within the community. Always consult your homeowner's association in the planning stage.

Beyond actual rules and regulations, basic courtesy dictates some aspects of the construction process. In all likelihood, you've decided to add on rather than move to a new house partly because you like your neighborhood.

So it's counterproductive to irritate your neighbors with thoughtless construction practices. Head off any potential confrontations with neighbors by letting them know—in person whenever possible—what your construction plans are. Noise being one of the chief complaints about any worksite, be sure that workers work only in the time frame specified in local building regulations (usually a typical 9-5 business day). If the project requires heavy equipment, try to schedule its use—such as the delivery and pour of concrete from a concrete truck—in the middle of the day. Also keep a clean worksite and take steps to prevent dirt or debris from migrating to a neighbor's property.

The Permit Process ▸

The process outlined below is typical of the steps involved in securing work permits for a large home-remodeling project such as a room addition. The process may differ slightly from locality to locality.

1. Submit application and plans with a contractor or architect (a licensed contractor may submit for you), and pay the application fee. Mechanical subcontractors may need separate permits.
2. Plans are reviewed for completeness and compliance with building codes.
3. Application and plans are forwarded to the zoning department for zone review.
4. Application and plans are approved.
5. Permit fee is paid and permit and inspection card are issued.
6. Site inspections occur as scheduled on the permit.
7. Completed project is inspected and approved, and a new certificate of occupancy is awarded where applicable.

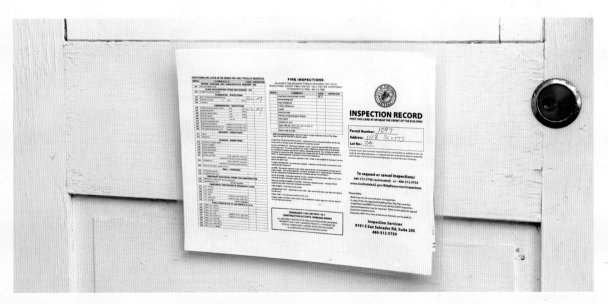

A job site inspection card must be posted in a visible location.

Drawing Construction Plans

Building plans are the roadmap for the journey that leads from that vision of a new and wonderful space in your head to the reality that you'll live with after the construction is completed. How closely the reality matches the vision depends on how detailed, concise, and comprehensive your addition building plans are.

The best way to begin the process is to sketch out a preliminary floor plan yourself. This is easily done with a few basic drafting supplies: a T-square or ruler, an adjustable triangle, grid paper, and a sharp pencil. Take measurements of the existing space that will connect to the addition, or that will be converted, and decide on the measurements of the new space. Now you can rough out the new space on the grid paper.

Use a standard scale of ¼ inch, ½ inch, or 1 inch to 1 foot and start from the exterior walls. Add the locations of doors (marking arcs for the door swing), windows, electrical outlets, plumbing fixtures, and other permanent features such as window seats. Think about where plumbing pipes and heating ducts will go. Finally, add interior walls.

One of the advantages to sketching your own preliminary drawings is that you can play with the dimensions, easily changing floor plan configurations and features to see which suits best. Concerned about light? Sketch in a bay or bow window. Suddenly realize the space is rather long and narrow? Break it up with a framed wall and doorway.

This exercise also gives you the chance to test furniture placement ideas. Cut top-view silhouettes out of construction paper or other thick stock, in shapes representing existing furniture you want to incorporate into the space or pieces you intend to buy. This is a great way to work out details of the floor plan, especially fixture and furniture placements that would present significant problems if discovered later in the construction process.

If you're more inclined to use a mouse than a pencil, you can try drafting your floor plan in one of the many computer-aided design (CAD) programs created just for homeowners. Unless you've had experience with these types of programs, you'll have to spend some time learning the software. However, working with software offers some unique and useful features such as calculating the amount of materials you'll need for the space you design.

Ultimately, no matter how good your drafting skills may be, you'll probably need professionally drawn plans to submit to the building department. Some municipalities allow homeowners to submit plans they've drawn, but most require professionally drafted blueprints and building plans. Although some contractors offer design services, for large, complex projects use an architect to draft your plans. You'll want to select someone who is familiar with the local building department and community.

Drawing preliminary floor plans is your chance to exercise your creativity, try different features and configurations, and get a sense of what the new space will look and feel like.

One of the other benefits of using an architect to create your plans is that he or she will also be able to make suggestions on structural issues you may not have considered.

Whoever drafts the plans will need to include the basic elements required by building departments. These usually entail blueprints that incorporate a site plan, floor plans, elevation drawings where applicable, and a materials list.

- **Site plans** show the addition in relation to the existing property, structures, and surrounding areas. These lay out important dimensions such as the lot size, distance from property setback lines and the position of the structure in relation to existing utilities.
- **Floor plans** are extremely accurate dimensional overviews that clearly show all relevant details such as exact location and dimensions of walls, windows, doors, plumbing, and electrical fixtures.
- **Elevation drawings** show the proposed addition from all sides. Elevation drawings sometimes include cutaway side views, depending on the requirements of the building department and the type of addition or conversion you're proposing.
- **A materials list** is included to show the building authorities that the construction will use only materials that conform to code. (It does not need to list quantities.)

As a collection of highly detailed drawings, the blueprints form specific instructions that you, the builder, and other professionals will follow in constructing the addition. That's why you'll need multiple copies of the blueprints. The building department usually requires that two or more copies be submitted with the permit application, and you'll want contractors and subcontractors to have copies depending on how involved they are (i.e., a plumber installing lines and fixtures for a kitchen and bath). Be sure to forward revised blueprints to everyone whenever changes are made after the initial blueprints are drafted.

A complete set of plans and blueprints drawn by a professional is the gold standard of home design and it will impress your local permit-issuing authorities. But a DIY package can be effective as long as it is put together neatly and with care and includes all of the required elements.

Project Scheduling

Scheduling a large project like a home addition, with all its stages and variables, can be quite a challenge. But if you get the details right and manage delays efficiently, you'll save yourself money, time, and frustration. If you're using a general contractor or architect, you can add the scheduling to their list of responsibilities. Even if you do, though, you should remain very involved in the process, reviewing the schedule and monitoring it as the project moves forward.

Whether you're setting the schedule or just policing it, you'll need to understand the steps and stages any addition project goes through. The first phase involves design and planning, gathering prices on materials, selecting the professionals who will be involved in the project, and navigating the permit process. This is followed by the preparation phase, when the actual schedule is drafted, permits are approved, and contracts are finalized. The last phase, the one for which the schedule is made, is the construction phase. That phase involves the following steps:

- **Foundation work.** Includes excavation, pouring and building the foundation, as well as installing drainage. Obviously, a garage or attic conversion won't usually require this step.
- **Framing.** Framing involves, in sequence, building the floor, raising walls, and attaching the roof. The same sequence applies to a conversion, only these stages usually involve reinforcing an existing framed structure.
- **Roofing.** Finishing the roof provides protection from the elements for work on the rest of the addition. Roofing includes the addition of dormers, skylights, or roof windows to an attic or garage.
- **Doors and windows.** This includes exterior and interior doors, as well as windows that are framed in new, or added into an existing wall, such as the side of a detached garage.
- **Exterior siding.** This involves both sheathing and adding housewrap to the walls, as well installing the final siding of choice. This is not usually an issue with attic conversions.

Create a comprehensive project schedule, making sure to use realistic time projections made with the input of any contractors who will be involved. Don't forget to allow for on-site building inspections required throughout the process. Inspectors generally will make a sincere effort to work within your schedule, but allow an extra day or two at each point.

- **Installing mechanicals.** Mechanicals include HVAC ducting and venting, plumbing runs, and electrical wiring.
- **Insulating.** Insulation is installed after all framing is in place and all ducts, wires, and pipes have been installed and inspected.
- **Finishing interior walls and ceiling.** This involves hanging drywall, taping and sanding joints and screws, and installing special surfaces such as a wood-paneled ceiling.
- **Flooring.** Final flooring can entail additional work if an underfloor heating system is to be used.
- **Trim and finish work.** Includes installation of moldings, plumbing and electrical fixtures, painting, and other finish details.

Scheduling these steps includes adding time for building inspections. You should also add room in the schedule for inevitable delays, the first of which is weather. You can head off some delays simply by ordering materials far in advance and storing them in a warm, dry area such as a garage. This not only ensures that the materials are there when needed, it also gives you a chance to inspect them and deal with breakage or delivery of the wrong materials without holding up construction.

How smoothly your schedule runs will also depend on the professionals you use. Never assume someone is going to show up when scheduled—always call to confirm. Staying in touch has a way of inspiring professionals to get their part of the project done. And encourage the professionals you use to communicate between themselves. If a contractor knows the electrician will be held up for a day, he may be able to schedule work on another part of the job.

Lastly, dealing with a schedule is an exercise in patience. Some delays simply can't be anticipated. People get sick, trucks break down, and you may even have a family emergency that shuts down construction for a few days. A little flexibility and expecting a surprise or two will go a long way toward maintaining your sanity and keeping the project on track.

Talk to Building Inspectors ▶

Although building inspectors aren't paid consultants, they can be an excellent design and planning resource. They are your community's field representatives, and their job is to inspect the work done on your project to ensure that it meets building code requirements.

As experts in their respective fields, the building inspector, electrical inspector, and plumbing inspector can give you sound advice on designing your kitchen. Not all inspectors have the time or the willingness to answer a lot of design questions, so make your questions short and specific, and be sure to describe your situation clearly. Also ask if the inspections office provides handouts that summarize the code requirements for common projects.

Flextime: Your Little Secret ▶

For added security, it's a good idea to add at least 25% more time to your best guess when determining the overall schedule for your remodeling project. Building in a few flex days as a safeguard against unforeseen problems is also a good idea. However, keep this information to yourself.

If contractors know that your schedule is padded, they may feel free to bump your project for a day or two to squeeze in a smaller rush job for another client. To ensure that your contractors stay on schedule, mark your flex days "cleanup" or "out of town"—don't tell them you've built some extra time into the schedule.

The Green Addition

The definition of "green" as it applies to home remodeling and construction is a matter of no small debate. And that definition will continue to change as new materials and technologies are developed and new legislation and regulations are set in place.

But certain universal principles drive any truly green remodeling. These include:

- **Energy efficiency.** The green movement at large deals with saving precious and non-renewable resources through energy conservation and by installing new sustainable technologies that exploit renewable energy sources such as photovoltaic electric panels or hydrothermal heating.
- **Resource conservation.** Truly green materials and processes use less natural resources than their predecessors, with a focus on conserving and recycling valuable, finite resources such as old-growth timber.

- **Environmental benefit.** A green technology or technique has minimal or no impact on the environment, or is a substitute for a much more ecologically damaging alternative.
- **Promotes a healthy home.** The best green options for your home bring the least amount of toxins and pollutants into your living space, helping keep you and your family healthy.

Building a green addition starts in the planning and design stage. The simplest way to minimize the addition's carbon footprint is to use the sun to your advantage. Orient your addition and its windows to take in a maximum of sunlight during the day, which reduces heating costs. Use other techniques to exploit the sun, such as reflective soffits that bounce warming sunlight in through windows, and operable awnings that can be opened to shade interior rooms and cool them down significantly in warmer seasons.

Solar energy collectors will add a green note to any room addition, but a truly green project involves many more design details that are not so obvious.

The purchase decisions you make will also have a dramatic effect on energy use. Select energy-efficient windows and doors to lessen the burden on the home's heating and air-conditioning systems. The greater expense up front will often be offset by energy savings in the long run. Choosing appliances and fixtures carefully is another way to cut down on energy usage. Look for the Energy Star label to select the most efficient, energy-conserving appliances.

The construction process itself presents vast opportunities to help the environment and conserve resources. Specify engineered or glue-laminated lumber for the main structural members in your addition, to conserve the number of trees that need to be cut down.

Wrap a building in a high-performance building wrap and specify the highest R-value insulation possible, given the type of framing you've chosen. These steps will help make the addition energy efficient.

You can go a step further with the help of modern technology. Install a passive solar system to heat water with the sun, or use photovoltaic panels to produce electricity for the space and the house at large. Solar panels often pay for themselves in a decade or less.

You can also take steps to minimize the impact of the construction on the environment and your family's health. Use flooring, paint, and surface finishes that emit low or no volatile organic compounds (VOCs) to improve air quality inside the space.

A Sampling of Green Building Products ▸

Some brands of interior-grade MDF panels are made from 100% recycled wood fibers and are manufactured with a synthetic resin containing no formaldehyde (see Resources, page 237).

Most of the big names in commercial paint offer high-performance synthetic paints in low-VOC formulations.

Natural paints are often made from plant sources, such as citrus fruits, tree resins, and seed oils.

Adhesives, spray products, paints, and other finishes with low emissions of toxic fumes are becoming commonplace on retail store shelves. Many are clearly labeled as green or low-VOC.

Cork, used to make these floor tiles, is a sustainable material because it's taken from trees every 10 years or so without harming the tree.

A green product on many counts, wood composite decking is made with post-consumer recycled plastic and wood fibers. It doesn't need toxic finishes for protection, and it outlasts solid-wood decking by a long shot.

No more free lunch. Mold-resistant drywall products limit mold growth by chemically treating or eliminating mold's favorite food: wet paper.

Portrait of a Green Kitchen

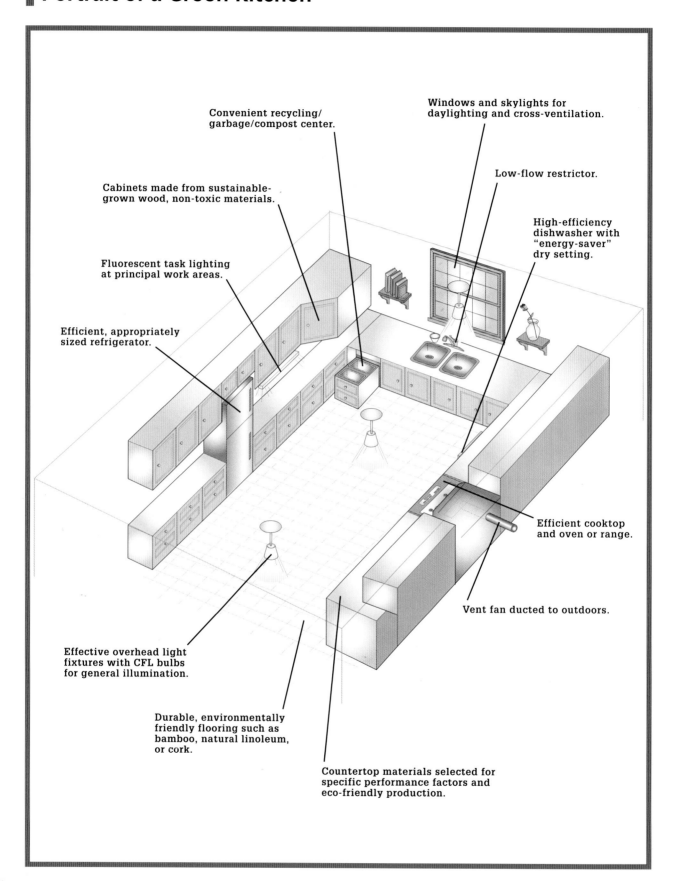

Convenient recycling/garbage/compost center.

Windows and skylights for daylighting and cross-ventilation.

Low-flow restrictor.

Cabinets made from sustainable-grown wood, non-toxic materials.

High-efficiency dishwasher with "energy-saver" dry setting.

Fluorescent task lighting at principal work areas.

Efficient, appropriately sized refrigerator.

Efficient cooktop and oven or range.

Effective overhead light fixtures with CFL bulbs for general illumination.

Vent fan ducted to outdoors.

Durable, environmentally friendly flooring such as bamboo, natural linoleum, or cork.

Countertop materials selected for specific performance factors and eco-friendly production.

Portrait of a Green Bathroom

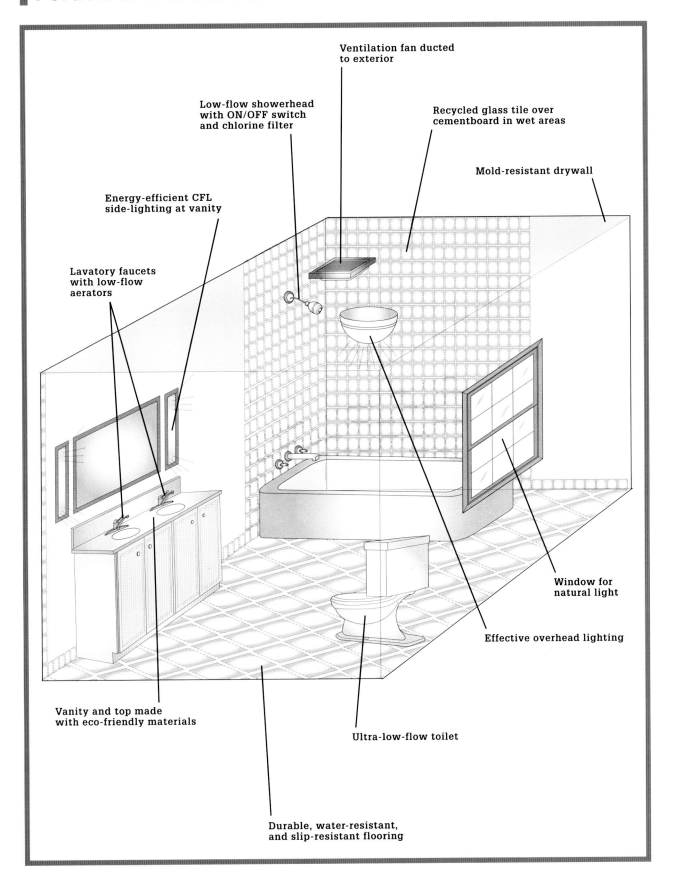

Ventilation fan ducted to exterior

Low-flow showerhead with ON/OFF switch and chlorine filter

Recycled glass tile over cementboard in wet areas

Mold-resistant drywall

Energy-efficient CFL side-lighting at vanity

Lavatory faucets with low-flow aerators

Window for natural light

Effective overhead lighting

Vanity and top made with eco-friendly materials

Ultra-low-flow toilet

Durable, water-resistant, and slip-resistant flooring

Preparing for Construction

Preparing your house and property for a new addition is a matter of setting the stage for the enormous work to come. Take pains to set up an orderly worksite and you will go a long way toward ensuring that the actual construction goes smoothly. The preparation for a project as complex as a home addition encompasses many tasks—creating access for workers and equipment, creating storage areas for materials, and providing a dumpster for the removal of waste materials.

Start preparing the worksite well in advance of the commencement of construction. You'll need to leave adequate time for preparation, particularly site preparation such as excavating and grading. In the case of a modest excavation for a slab base, you might opt to do the work yourself. If, however, the project entails a full basement foundation, you'll more likely need to schedule in professionals to dig the basement and footing trench.

The other steps involved in preparation are easy to manage alone or with a helper. Proper preparation heads off problems and is a critical step toward making sure your addition project runs smoothly.

In this chapter:

- Site Preparation
- Laying Out a Room Addition Foundation
- Worksite Safety & Security
- Excavating the Site

Site Preparation

Before the construction activity gets underway in earnest you should make some site preparations to ensure reasonable access to the work area, as well as to protect your house and grounds from the inevitable stresses of a major construction project. Readying your building site entails moving features and fixtures that are within the borders of the actual job site or the path workers will use to move materials, equipment, and building waste in and out of the work area.

Start by moving the manmade structures. These include outdoor furnishings such as patio tables and chairs, umbrellas, planters, playsets and sandboxes, statuary, and garden ornaments. Prevent any chance of damage by storing these far from the work site, ideally in a protected space such as a garage or shed. In some cases, providing access to the worksite requires removing a fence—temporarily at least.

Remove landscape features as necessary to make runs in parallel construction. Completing a room addition that increases the footprint of your house usually requires that you relocate or remove a landscape feature or two. If a tree or shrub is too large to be moved, you can either remove it, protect it—such as wrapping the trunk of a tree in used tires—or relocate it. You can actually plan the relocation of a tree or large bush as part of the excavation process; a backhoe can do in minutes what might take hours or even days to accomplish by hand. When considering the plants on your lot, begin by looking upward. The altered roofline of a room addition or attic conversion may run right into a large tree branch. It's wise to remedy the situation before, rather than in the middle of construction.

How to Limb a Tree ▸

The best tool for pruning is a telephone. Use it to call an arborist and have them assess the tree and make the appropriate cuts. If you do decide to go it alone, be careful, and follow these basic rules:

- Never cut away more than ⅓ of the tree's branches.
- Start with a shallow undercut several inches away from the branch bark collar—the bulge where the branch meets the trunk. The undercut ensures the bark doesn't peel off as the branch drops.
- Complete the cut from the top to remove the bulk of the branch.
- Make a final cut flush with the outside of the branch bark collar. Do not cut into the collar.
- Leave the wound to heal itself. Don't paint it or add any kind of sealant or preservative.

Start by undercutting from beneath the limb with your bow saw or chain saw.

Finish the cut from above—this keeps the bark from tearing when the limb breaks loose.

Trim the stub from the limb so it's flush with the branch collar.

Mark underground utilities such as gas and water lines prior to beginning any project that involves digging. Even if lines are indicated on your original plan drawings or site survey, contact the local utilities (call 811) and have them come out to flag the exact location of all lines that are anywhere near the building site. Technicians from the utilities will visit your site and identify the location of underground lines for free.

Mark your property boundaries, whether or not you are expanding outward. Even a small attic conversion will mean a lot of traffic through your yard, with a high potential that pallets of materials will be stationed temporarily on the ground. Marking property lines helps ensure that neither you nor your workers causes any damage to your neighbor's property.

Prepare the interior of the work site, especially if there will be substantial work done inside, as with an attic conversion. Line the pathway in and out of the house by taping down heavy-duty kraft paper from the work area to the nearest exit. You'll also want to partition off any area or room in the house that might be affected by work debris such as dust from sanding drywall joints. Use double layers of thick plastic sheeting to separate the worksite from other areas in the home.

Have all utility lines flagged and marked with spray paint before you dig. Utility companies provide this service free of charge. There is now a national toll-free number in the United States you can call to get referrals for free flagging of utility lines (call 811).

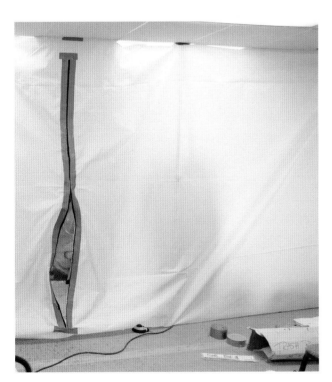

Erect temporary walls to create barriers between the work area and the rest of your house. Heavy duty plastic sheeting is best for this.

Clear the area around the building site to create a staging ground for building materials and temporary storage for excavated dirt. Arrange to have dirt removed as soon as possible. A temporary fence such as a snow fence is required around excavation areas by some codes.

Laying Out a Room Addition Worksite

Precise foundation measurements are essential to ensuring that a room addition aligns exactly with the existing house structure. If the measurements are off by even a modest amount, floors and walls may not line up and the transition from old space to new will not be as seamless and fluid as it should be.

The first and most exacting step in building the addition's foundation is laying out a series of level "string lines" attached to the existing foundation and defining the outside boundaries of the new foundation. (Nylon string is used because cotton lines can stretch and sag.) These lines will guide the placement of trench footings and foundation walls, and they indicate the exact height to which the foundation is to be poured or laid.

Determining the correct height for the string lines can be more complex than simply lining them up with the height of the old foundation. Older lumber is,

in many cases, different dimensions than the same lumber cut to modern "nominal" dimensions. This means that the floor structure in an older home may differ significantly from the dimensions of a new floor constructed in exactly the same way. Consequently, you'll need to measure the existing floor structure, compare it to the total measurement of the floor you intend to build for the addition, and adjust the height of the new foundation to accommodate any differences between the two.

The walls of an older home may also be out of square and plumb, complicating the layout of your new foundation. If this is the case, the string lines will help you visualize the space and make it easier to decide whether to lay out the foundation perfectly square or adjust the measurements to account for the variation, so that it better fits with the existing house.

How to Lay Out a Square Foundation

Measure along the ledger board and mark the distance in from the edges of the finished room to the centers of the beam support posts, according to your plan (this presumes post-and-beam construction; if you are pouring a concrete footing, mark the outer edges of the footings on the ledger).

Drive a 10d nail into the bottom edge of the ledger to make a fastening point for your layout strings. Tie a layout string securely to the nail.

Build four barter boards and drive the first into the ground so the center is aligned with the post location on the ledger (inset). The batter board should be 18 to 24" past the edge of the project area. Tie the free end of the mason's string to the crosspiece on the batterboard (once the strings are squared up you will drive a nail at the correct point to tie off the string). Use a framing square at the ledger to establish the rough position of the string.

Adjust the string so it is exactly perpendicular to the ledger. Use the 3-4-5 method of measuring, and move the string on the crosspiece of the batterboards until it is square. Repeat this process for a string to mark the other side of the project area. Measure the distance between the strings on the batterboards: it should be the same as the distance between strings on the ledger.

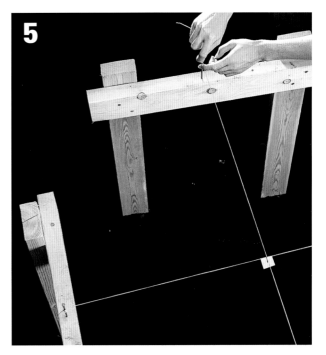

Install batterboards to tie off the mason's string marking the front edge of the addition (if you're pouring concrete) or the centerpoints of the support posts (post and beam).

(continued)

Measure the diagonals on the layout to confirm that the lines are square. Adjust and readjust the lines until all corners are exactly square—even if the front and back distances are equal the lines may not be square, so check carefully. Also use a line level to make sure all lines have no slope—this too could throw off your layout.

Use masking tape to stick the lines together where they meet at the corners and then measure and tape the locations for additional post centers along the lines (if you're pouring a footing you can skip this step).

Hang a plumb bob from each taped point and transfer the location to the ground. Drive a small stake or a landscape spike at each location. You'll need to remove the lines to excavate for posts or footings, but keep the batterboards in position if possible in case you need to re-establish your locations.

Removing Siding ▸

Many additions require that you remove all of the siding in the building area. New interior walls inside the addition should be attached to wall studs, not installed over siding. For accurate layout measurements, this means it is often necessary to remove the siding before you establish your project lines. With some additions, such as a three-season porch, it may be necessary to remove the siding only where the wall framing members for the addition will attach to the house. Do not remove exterior wall coverings until you have a means for sealing the wall (usually a tarp tucked under the top siding lap and fastened to the wall).

Create cutting lines on the wall by measuring and marking the locations of the addition walls on the existing siding. Use a level and straightedge as guides for marking the lines. Cut enough to leave room for sheathing and inside corner trim, if necessary.

Cut lap siding with a circular saw (a cordless trim saw is a great choice). Set the blade cutting depth to match the thickness of the material you're cutting, which may or may not include the wall sheathing. *Tip: Many pros prefer to cut vinyl siding with the blade installed backwards. This still cuts through the material with ease, but with less chance of tearing the siding.*

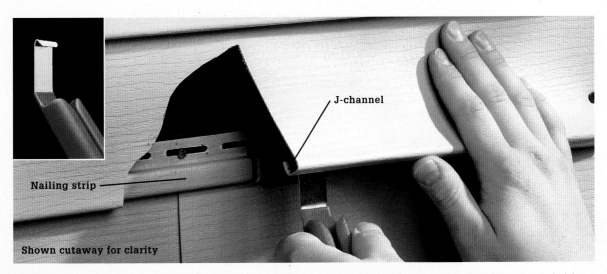

Nailing strip

J-channel

Shown cutaway for clarity

Vinyl and metal siding panels have a locking J-channel that fits over the bottom of the nailing strip on the underlying piece. Use a zip-lock tool (inset) to separate panels. Insert the tool at the seam nearest the repair area. Slide it over the J-channel, pulling outward slightly, to unlock the joint from the siding below.

Worksite Safety & Security

Every construction site poses dangers and risks, and it's no different when the site is your home. That's why an important part of getting your addition built is ensuring not only the safety of you and your family, but also taking steps to make sure workers and their equipment are protected. This isn't just the conscientious thing to do; it's also the best way to limit your liability from any accidents or damage that might occur during construction. And ultimately, a safe and secure work site is the most efficient and economical site.

There are many safety factors to deal with in construction as complex as a home addition. But it all starts with a clear staging area.

A staging area is simply a clearly identified location away from the construction, used for tool and equipment storage and perhaps for some strategizing. The best staging area has a clear, flat square where materials can be laid out and inspected or organized. It should also have power close enough to be reached with an extension cord, so that power tools such as saws can be set up to prepare materials for installation. A worktable—even if it is only a sheet of plywood across two sawhorses—can be a great staging area feature, providing a centralized location to study plans, discuss strategies, and meet with key players such as building inspectors.

Staging areas also help organize tools and equipment. Providing a single location for valuable tools and equipment helps keep them from being mislaid. Of course, tools can go missing for other reasons as well, which is why any decent staging area includes a locked storage capacity.

Proper safety gear and practices are just as essential as a place for tools and equipment. Practice safety whenever you're working on the site, and require any workers on the site to do the same. In particular, make sure everyone wears safety eyewear when power tools or equipment are in operation, and inspect those tools—even if they're not yours—to see that the appropriate chain, motor, and blade guards are in place. As the homeowner, don't take your liability and exposure lightly.

Construction waste disposal is another issue affecting not only work site safety, but the larger matter of homeowner liability. Obviously, any debris scattered about a work site increases the potential for injury. That's why project preparation must include planning for efficient waste disposal. On larger projects, this will probably involve a dumpster provided and serviced by a dedicated construction waste disposal company. On smaller projects, getting rid of waste usually involves the homeowner or contractor hauling the debris to a dump site. Either way, know how and when construction debris and other waste will be removed, where it will be stored before removal, and how waste disposal is budgeted. You should also make arrangements for disposal of any hazardous or toxic materials.

Providing the proper facilities is a way of securing the rest of your home. The vast majority of contractors and professionals are scrupulously honest,

Handling Dangerous Waste ▸

The construction process creates two types of dangerous waste materials, both of which must be handled carefully and correctly.

- **Toxic materials** such as asbestos or lead paint need to be removed or treated according to prevailing law and ordinances. This usually involves hiring an abatement professional or a certified contractor. As part of the process, the professional either seals the material or strips and removes it, disposing of the waste according to established guidelines. While

some localities do allow homeowners to remove asbestos and lead paint, safety authorities strongly discourage it as a DIY practice.

- **Hazardous materials** are a trickier type of waste. These include common construction debris such as partial cans of paint and caulking, and more potent trash such as thermostat switches that contain mercury, fluorescent light bulbs or fixture ballasts, and old appliances containing PCBs. Consult local environmental authorities, usually found in the solid waste management department of your municipality.

but it never hurts to take precautions. Lock areas of the home you don't want workers entering, and if you prefer that workers not eat or take breaks in the house or addition space, identify a location (preferably with some protection against sun and inclement weather) where they can take breaks. If you don't want workers using your bathroom, you should arrange for a portable toilet.

Working Safely

Use a GFCI extension cord when working outdoors. GFCIs (ground-fault circuit-interrupters) shut off power if a short circuit occurs.

Use cordless tools to eliminate the hazards of extension cords, especially when working from ladders.

Use fiberglass or wood ladders when working near power cables. Exercise extreme caution around these cables, and only work near them when absolutely necessary.

Never climb a ladder with a loaded air nailer attached to a pressurized air hose. Even with trigger safeties, air guns pose a serious danger to the operator as well as anyone who may be standing near the ladder.

Using Scaffolding

Steel tubular scaffolding is available from any rental center for daily, weekly, or monthly rates. Begin by setting up the scaffolding on flat ground, free from mud and construction debris. If you have to adjust the first level for uneven terrain, follow the instructions carefully. Do not use stacks of boards or cinder blocks to create a level surface.

Each stage of scaffolding consists of two end frames, several crossbraces, and planking that makes up the platform. Set up the first level of scaffolding on steel base plates, if your equipment has them, or on wide wood base supports. Use string lines and bubble levels to make sure the end frames are level and plumb. If the scaffolding has screw jack adjusters, use them to level the structure.

Make sure all the components are fully seated in their joints, then add the planking to create the first platform. The platform shouldn't sway. Platform planks should line up evenly to prevent tripping hazards. Keep gaps between the planks to 1 inch or less. Once the first level of staging is secure, repeat the process to build the second stage of scaffold. Make sure any connective locking pins are securely engaged from one stage to the next. If you need to build scaffolding more than 16 feet high, use wall brackets that clamp to the scaffold and bolt them into solid wall framing for added stability. No matter how high your scaffold becomes, it must remain as stable as the first stage. Add any guard rails, end rails, or toe boards that may be required.

Using scaffolding is by far the safest way to work on exterior walls and roofs. Rental is relatively affordable, and you can usually get a better deal if you're using it for a week or longer.

How to Set Up Scaffolding

Clear the setup area of debris, and then assemble the first two end frames and crossbraces to create the bottom stage of scaffold framing.

Use string lines and levels to check end frames for level and plumb. Adjust the structure using screw jacks mounted to the frame legs, or by a leveling technique recommended by the manufacturer. The end-frame legs should rest firmly on wood or steel base plates. Never use stacks of boards or cinder blocks for leveling purposes. Lay the planks in position to form the bottom platform.

Assemble the parts for the second stage on top of the first stage. Make sure all joints and connective locking pins are fully engaged from one stage to the next.

Excavating the Site

Although you could easily argue that it is part of the actual construction project, excavating the site is also a form of preparation. Just make sure you're pretty much set to go before you begin digging. The goal is to leave the excavation open for as short a time as possible.

If you'll be laying a simple slab foundation, you may be able to complete the digging yourself using hand digging tools. But in most cases, where the foundation will include a crawl space or full basement, you should employ professional help and some heavy machinery. This usually means a backhoe or a similar piece of earthmoving equipment, as well as a qualified operator. If you've done a good job in setting up the site, the driver will have plenty of room to navigate around the dig. You'll also need to plan for dirt removal. Although you may be able to use some of the soil to backfill and grade other areas of your property, you'll probably need to have a significant amount trucked offsite.

The digging itself requires more than just burrowing a big hole. It's essential to check the depth as the digging proceeds because the goal is to set a level base for the footing at precisely the depth you need it. Most codes do not allow you to backfill a foundation excavation, so digging too deep can mean paying for special backfill material and processes.

The sides of the foundation are usually cut square to the floor. But the walls may need be cut at angles if the soil is sandy or prone to crumbling, or if room is needed for drainage or waterproofing on the outside of the foundation. Removing dirt along the existing foundation wall can occasionally reveal an unpleasant surprise, such as a buckling section that requires buttressing. But usually, if you've been careful in the excavation, you'll have a level accessible hole in which to place your footing and foundation walls.

Call in the heavy equipment if you are excavating for a full basement. Not only will it save a monumental amount of labor, but a professional backhoe operator is far less likely to create collateral damage than a homeowner.

Foundations

The main purpose of any foundation is to stabilize and secure the structure. But in the case of an addition, the foundation is also the first and most substantial connection of the new space to the old. Any new foundation must not only serve the structure of the addition, it must also make the link with the main building seamless and structurally invisible.

One of the key initial decisions that you or the professionals you hire will need to make is to choose the foundation type. The best choice will depend on many factors but is ultimately driven by engineering issues. That's why the foundation is one of the many stages in building an addition in which the advice of qualified professionals can be indispensable.

Whatever type of foundation you wind up using for your particular addition, precise measurements are very important. A correctly dimensioned foundation is vital to guaranteeing that all the other structural elements line up correctly with what's already there. The choice of foundation also affects what type of waterproofing, drainage, and insulation you can and should install.

In this chapter:

- Choosing a Foundation
- Pouring a Footing
- Tying Into an Existing Foundation
- Laying a Concrete Block Foundation
- Installing a Poured Concrete Foundation
- Waterproofing Foundation Walls
- Insulating Foundations
- Framing the Floor

Choosing a Foundation

No single type of foundation is appropriate for every addition. The one you choose will depend on many different factors, including the existing foundation of your home, your budget, your local climate and soil conditions, and others. If you carefully weigh the strengths and weaknesses of different foundations against the particular characteristics of your project, one foundation type should emerge as the obvious choice.

Foundations require a stable base (usually called a footing) that functions as a sort of foundation for the foundation. Building codes clearly designate footing dimensions and depth in relationship to the width and height of the foundation wall; the footing is usually at least twice as wide as the wall, and twice as deep as the wall is wide. This is because the footing is critical in evenly distributing the weight of the foundation and addition.

Footing code requirements take into account several key issues, but the most significant are frostline considerations. The frostline is the depth to which the soil in your area regularly freezes during the winter. Because freezing temperatures cause soil movement that can strain and potentially crack concrete structures, building codes dictate how far footings (and sometimes foundation walls) must extend below grade—usually 12 inches or more below the official frostline depth for the area. Anyone working on the foundation should know these code requirements. Although that will most likely be a professional, you may want to tackle the job yourself if you've opted for a more basic type of foundation.

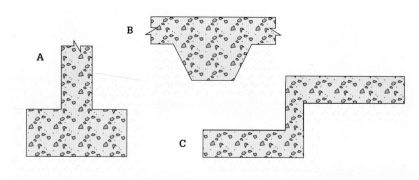

Three of the many possibilities for designing a footing for your addition foundation include: a spread footing (A); an interior load-bearing wall footing (B); a step footing (C).

Frost line

Footing size and depth are structural issues that are dictated by local codes. The codes take into account local climate conditions. Consult your building inspector for requirements in your area.

Foundation Types

The following descriptions represent some of the most common foundation types.

A slab-on-grade is the most basic foundation and usually the simplest to build. The foundation consists of a concrete slab laid directly on leveled ground, and the footings are usually poured at the same time as the slab. A layer of sand or gravel covered with a thick sheet of polyethylene forms a moisture barrier beneath the slab. In cooler climates rigid insulation is laid over the gravel, and against the inside wall. The footings are reinforced with rebar, as is the slab, although sometimes wire mesh is used depending on the thickness of the foundation (slabs are generally between 4 inches and 8 inches thick). But even with the reinforcement, these foundations are susceptible to freeze-and-thaw soil movement unless they are insulated, which is why they are generally used only in temperate areas of the country or beneath smaller, stand-alone structures like sheds. The placement of utilities is also a challenge. Wiring, plumbing, and HVAC ductwork will have to run through walls or ceilings, or special steps will need to be taken to route lines through the slab. Slabs are also inappropriate for some types of flooring, so you should always consult a professional to determine if the flooring you want to use will work over this foundation. Like many foundations, slabs are most efficient when married to a similar foundation. If the house itself is not on a slab, you may have to accommodate a variation in height between the addition and the house. *Note: Some kind of foundation insulation is required by code in most areas.*

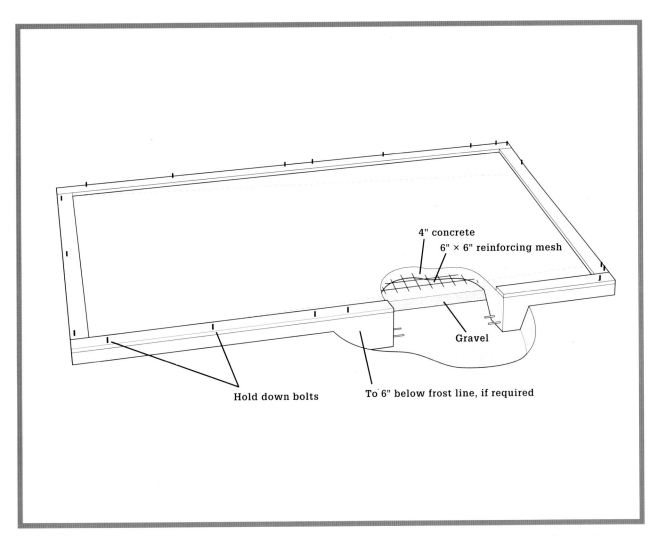

4" concrete

6" × 6" reinforcing mesh

Gravel

Hold down bolts

To 6" below frost line, if required

A slab-on-grade foundation is used most often with standalone structures like sheds and garages. In some climates with no frostline restrictions, slabs may be used as foundations for attached additions.

Perimeter wall foundations can be constructed of poured concrete or concrete block. Once in place they create a crawl space that is normally at least 24 inches high. The crawl space is left unfinished, with a bare earth floor and walls completely covered with a polyethylene vapor barrier and rigid insulation to prevent moisture-related problems such as rot and mold. The crawl space allows room for air circulation and allows you to run utilities under the floor even after the foundation has been laid. The floor support for a perimeter wall foundation can be constructed one of two ways. Usually, traditional joists are set on the mudsills that line the top of the walls and are tied into the existing floor structure. But where additional support is necessary, a pier or cutout can be incorporated into each side of the foundation (sometimes supplemented by a center pier and post), to support a beam. Perimeter wall crawl spaces were traditionally vented to prevent moisture build-up, but recent research suggests that lining the floor and walls with rigid insulation is more effective. In any case, this type of foundation is far less expensive than a full basement, but can't match the basement's insulating and space potential. That's why perimeter wall foundations are most common in warmer parts of the country and for smaller additions.

Full basements are the most spacious, usable, and energy-efficient foundation option, but they are also the most complex, time consuming, and expensive to build. A basement includes walls of poured concrete or concrete block that run far below the frost line. A concrete slab is poured to serve as the floor of the basement. The thickness of the basement walls depends on their actual height and local codes, although 8 to 12 inches is most common. This is the most challenging type of foundation to build, but it offers several advantages, not the least of which is its exceptional load-bearing capacity. In the case of an extensive addition with multiple rooms including plumbed and wired fixtures, the basement can house dedicated utilities such as a supplemental water heater. The basement itself can also serve as living space, effectively increasing the square footage of the addition. Basement space insulates the floor above from temperature variations so that the floor in the addition is always comfortable underfoot. Basements are most popular in the colder areas of the country where they provide support well below the frost line, but are applicable to any addition that could put the extra space to good use. However, if the existing house has a shallow foundation, additional costs will be incurred for building a support wall so that the existing foundation isn't undercut.

A perimeter wall foundation has concrete or block walls that are laid and poured only to crawlspace depth.

A full basement requires a full-height foundation wall around the entire perimeter of the addition.

Post-and-pier is a less common foundation consisting of several independent piers that are essentially substantial concrete footings anchoring vertical "posts." The posts, in turn, support beams (which is why this foundation is sometimes called "pier-and-beam") that form the underlying floor structure for the addition. Although inexpensive and relatively simple to construct, post-and-pier foundations are not as strong as other types, especially when it comes to torsional (side-to-side) forces such as high winds or earthquakes. Local codes in some areas may prohibit post-and-pier foundations; consequently, their use has traditionally been limited to specialized situations such as a steeply sloped yard where it would be impractical to use another type of foundation. The piers themselves can be precast and set in place at the site, poured on site, or built up from concrete blocks. The posts are either pressure-treated wood or metal and are embedded in the structure of the pier or attached to it by metal brackets. One of the main benefits of a post-and-pier foundation is that it provides maximum access to the underside of the addition, making the placement of utilities and ventilation ducting a very simple process. Post-and-pier foundations are often used to elevate houses along rivers or other areas prone to flooding.

Permanent Wood Foundations (PWF) are an alternative to either a perimeter wall or full basement foundations. The walls are built on a gravel footing and are constructed in the same manner as any other framed wall, except that both the framing members and plywood sheathing are specially treated with long-lasting preservative. Because insulation can be installed in the wood framed wall cavity, the PWF can be warmer than a concrete foundation wall. A PWF generally is easier and cheaper to build than other types of foundations. It also has better access for running utilities and for finishing the space. However, a wood foundation must be more carefully built than concrete or block and more carefully protected against moisture and termites.

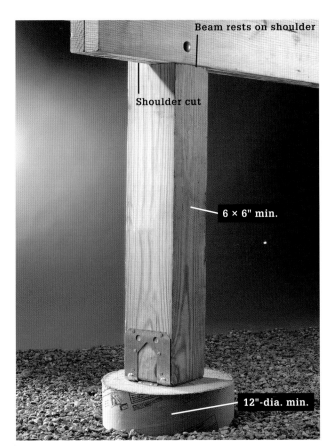

Beam rests on shoulder

Shoulder cut

6 × 6" min.

12"-dia. min.

Post and pier foundations are sometimes used for additions, often to accommodate a steep slope.

Permanent wood foundations are built using lumber and wood sheet goods that are pressure-treated with preservative and rated for ground contact.

Pouring a Footing

An addition foundation is laid in stages, each stage building on the previous one. The process starts with excavation of the foundation hole and leveling of the grade on which the foundation will stand. Then the trench for the footing—the solid base for everything that comes after—is dug, and the footing is laid. Finally, the walls are laid or poured and the floor constructed in preparation for the main structure of the addition. If the foundation is developed correctly, the rest of the addition will mesh fluidly with, and last as long as, the existing structure.

The footing is the least visible part of the whole structure, but it's an essential underpinning nonetheless. The footing trench is marked using a plumb line in reference to the corners defined by your original string lines. The trench needs to accommodate a footing that's typically twice as wide as the wall that stands on it, and twice as deep as the wall is wide. The footing can be poured into a cleanly cut trench or, if the soil is not that stable, form boards can be used.

With the footing in place, forms are positioned or, if you're laying a concrete block wall, that process is begun. In either case, the first step is tying into the existing foundation, usually with rebar "pins" that are affixed in holes drilled into the existing foundation. The addition's foundation walls are reinforced throughout, and the floor of the crawlspace or basement is completed with a vapor barrier and, in the case of a basement, a slab. Finally, the floor is built, setting the stage on which the rest of the room addition will take shape.

Tools & Materials ▸

Spade or square- edged shovel	2 × 4s
Sledgehammer	Vegetable oil
Cordless drill	Metal tie wires
Bolsters or bricks	No. 4 rebar
	Steel stakes

A concrete footing provides a flat, sturdy surface on which you can stack concrete block foundation walls or pour concrete walls.

How to Prepare a Footing Trench

Dig the trench to the plan-specified depth and width. Use a square-end spade to smooth and square the sides of the trench. Thoroughly compact the floor of the trench with a tamper.

Frame the top of the trench with 2 × 4 form lumber. Drive stakes next to the 2 × 4 form boards and attach the boards to the stakes (the round steel stakes seen here are predrilled for deck screws). Level the form boards side-to-side and along their lengths.

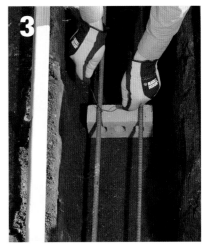

Reinforce the footing with No. 4 re-bar. Set the rebar on bricks, stones, or use rebar bolsters to raise the rods off the bottom of the trench.

Bind the rebar with metal tie wires to keep the parallel rods from separating when the concrete is poured. Installing a few spacers between rods to keep them separated is also a good idea.

Drive sections of rebar, at least 24" long, into the ground vertically, every 4 ft. and at least 1 ft. from corners. Position the vertical rebar so it will fall in the void areas of concrete blocks. Fill the forms with concrete.

Tying Into an Existing Foundation

Connecting a new foundation for an addition onto the existing house foundation is an engineering requirement. If you don't physically couple the two foundations, sooner or later you may end up with two separate buildings. By linking the two foundations you take a big step toward ensuring that the construction is structurally sound.

The traditional technique for tying in the new foundation to the old is to drill holes in the existing mating wall, insert rebar "pins" 6 inches to 8 inches deep, securing them in the concrete with epoxy glue. Then it's just a matter of grafting the exposed rebar ties to full lengths of rebar that are installed to reinforce the new foundation when you set up the forms.

This technique was developed for poured foundations, but can also be used with other types. When laying a new foundation of concrete block walls, you can either drill the end blocks to accept the epoxied pins, or you can use special blocks with cavities meant just for this purpose. As you add each course and slip the end blocks onto the pins, tie them to rebar rods positioned vertically through the holes in the blocks, and fill the holes with concrete.

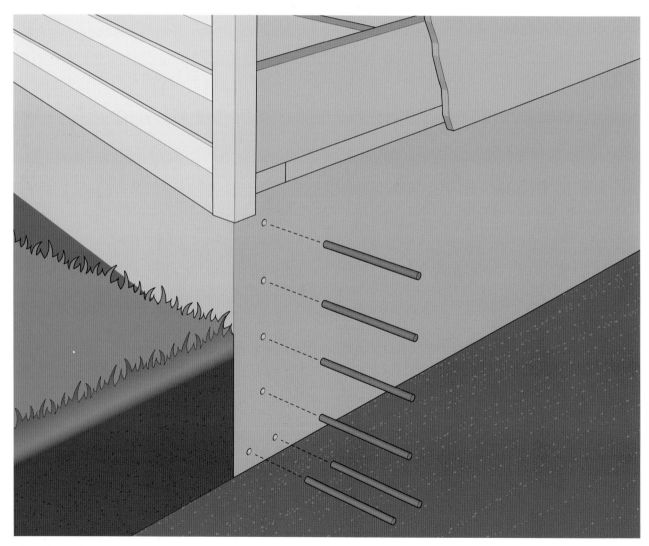

Tie rods cut from no. 4 rebar, usually around 8 to 10" in length, are inserted into holes drilled into the foundation wall and then secured with epoxy glue. The free ends of the tie rods are bound to full-length rebar rods with tie wire.

Tie-in Challenges ▶

In some situations, the traditional method of tying a new foundation wall to an existing one isn't going to work. For instance, if your new foundation wall abuts a concrete block foundation, the existing foundation may be hollow at the points you want to drive the rebar in and set it. If this is the case, you'll have to use one of the many masonry fasteners available (after consulting your local building department for code restrictions, of course). One example is a vertical ladder of fastener strips that are screwed into the existing wall with masonry screws, and locked into the new wall by means of arms that project horizontally from the mounting strips. You'll find other types of wall ties suited to different situations at masonry supply stores. As a last resort—and only if code allows—you can line the joint between the two walls with waterproof expansion material just as you would a large concrete slab. Once the new wall is in place, the joint will tolerate a certain amount of movement while still maintaining a waterproof seal.

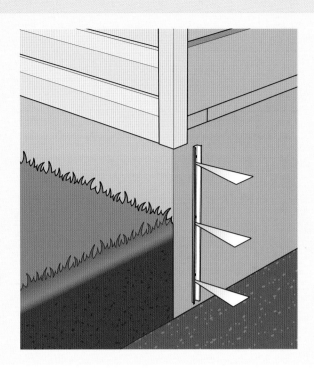

Tying Into Concrete

Use a corded hammer drill with a ½" or ⅝" masonry bit to drill access holes for the No. 4 rebar tie rods. Drilling concrete can be a slow job, but do not get impatient and lean too hard on the drill—let the bit do the work.

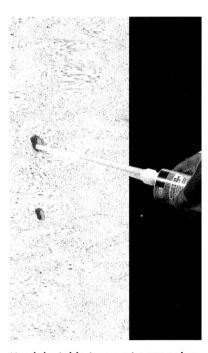

Use injectable two-part epoxy glue to secure the ends of the rebar tie rods into the holes drilled in your existing foundation wall. Make sure the concrete dust is all cleared from the hole before injecting glue and inserting rods.

Laying a Concrete Block Foundation

Building a concrete block foundation wall is a project even the unskilled home handyman can tackle, because the skills needed are minimal and can be honed through practice. The chief requirement in laying this type of foundation is careful attention to detail, beginning with the measurements.

Although it may seem counterintuitive, the best way to measure for a concrete block wall is from the top down. If you've laid out your string lines correctly, you've already determined the top-of-foundation height; ideally you want the distance down to the footing to equal an exact number of block courses (which, with standard blocks, will be a multiple of 8). Once you've got the measurement right, you can help yourself by working slowly and methodically and following some time-tested rules. When it comes to mortar, be conservative. You should only mix the mortar you'll use in about thirty minutes; if mortar sits around longer than that

it will become difficult to work with. If you're having problems, don't hesitate to mix a new batch of mortar—it should be just stiff enough so that it's not runny. Toss old mortar down the cavities of the wall. Beyond that, follow the steps here and you'll build a sound, plumb and level foundation for your room addition.

Tools & Materials ▸

Circular saw with	Level
masonry blade	Mason's jointer
Mason's chisel and maul	Mortar
Sledgehammer	1 × 1 piece
Masonry hoe	No. 4 rebar
Trowel	Steel ladder braces

Buttering a concrete block involves laying narrow slices of mortar on the two flanges at the end of the block. It is not necessary to butter the valley between the flanges unless the project calls for it.

How to Cut Concrete Block

Mark cutting lines on both faces of the block, and then score ⅛ to ¼"-deep cuts along the lines using a circular saw equipped with a masonry blade.

Use a mason's chisel and maul to split one face of the block along the cutting line. Turn the block over and split the other face.

Option: Cut half blocks from combination corner blocks. Corner blocks have preformed cores in the center of the web. Score lightly above the core, and then rap with a mason's chisel to break off half blocks.

How to Mix Mortar

Empty mortar mix into a mortar box and form a depression in the center. Add about ¾ of the recommended amount of water into the depression, and then mix it in with a masonry hoe. Do not overwork the mortar. Continue adding small amounts of water and mixing until the mortar reaches the proper consistency. Do not mix too much mortar at one time—mortar is much easier to work with when it is fresh.

Set a piece of plywood on blocks at a convenient height, and place a shovelful of mortar onto the surface. Slice off a strip of mortar from the pile using the edge of your mason's trowel. Slip the trowel point-first under the section of mortar and lift up.

Snap the trowel gently downward to dislodge excess mortar clinging to the edges. Position the trowel at the starting point, and "throw" a line of mortar onto the building surface. Do not get ahead of yourself. If you throw too much mortar, it will set before you are ready.

How to Build a Block Foundation Wall

Position story poles at each corner of the foundation. Mark the top line using the string lines as reference, and then mark down 8" for each course of blocks.

Lay the first course in a "dry run" to determine if you'll need to cut or use any special blocks. Use a scrap piece ⅜" thick as a spacer for the mortar joints.

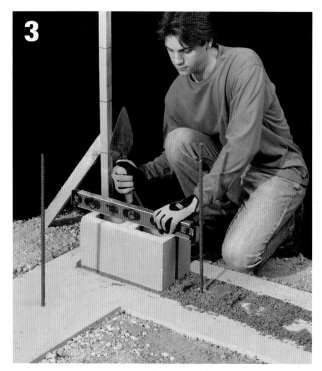

Lay the first block by spreading enough mortar for three blocks in a ladder pattern. Set the corner block in place and check plumb and level against the story pole.

Set the opposite corner block in place and position mason line blocks and guide string. Follow the string in laying the rest of the course.

As you build courses, tie supporting rebar to the footing rebar. Fill the rebar cavities with concrete.

Cut blocks as necessary, scoring on your mark and breaking with a hammer and broad cold chisel. You can also use a grinder equipped with a diamond blade.

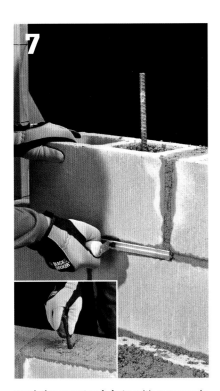

Tool the mortar joints with a mason's jointer when the mortar is "thumbprint" ready. Sink anchor bolts for the mudsill into block cavities filled with concrete (inset). Space them roughly every 4 ft.

Provide additional lateral reinforcement by using steel truss work braces or "ladders" made to lay across the top of a course around the block cavities. These should be used every other course for best effect. Lastly, you can use special metal lath to isolate a course and fill just that course with concrete—a requirement of some codes for the top-most course.

Installing a Poured Concrete Foundation

Pouring concrete foundation walls requires more setup than building one out of concrete blocks. But even given the extra preparation, a poured foundation actually takes less time to complete. However, just as when laying concrete block, pouring a sound foundation requires attention to detail and proper reinforcement.

The focus is on the form preparation because wet concrete doesn't provide much margin for error. Once you begin pouring the concrete, it's hard to correct mistakes. Because the foundation is all of a piece, a single mistake on one wall can compromise the entire foundation. Even a simple problem can wreak havoc with your schedule and budget. So it pays to carefully construct strong, stable forms, the first line of defense against pricey, time-consuming problems.

Forms are the molds for the foundation walls. They are a series of interlinked units that are constructed to be exceptionally strong—freshly poured concrete is a dense, flowing mass that exerts powerful pressure on any surface it contacts. To counteract that pressure, forms are commonly built of sturdy ¾-inch, smooth exterior grade plywood with a supporting structure, usually made from 2 × 4s. There are many

ways to actually construct a form—for instance, boards are sometimes used in place of plywood—but all forms have the same goal: to hold their position under intense pressure, maintaining uniform wall thickness while the concrete dries and sets.

Building and positioning the forms is the most time-consuming part of the process; pouring and finishing the concrete rarely takes more than an hour or so. If you don't have any "blowouts" in which one or more forms are compromised, the forms are simply removed after a few days, once the concrete has completely set.

Tools & Materials ▸

¾" plywood sheets	Cordless drill
2 × 4s	Stringer
No. 3 rebar	Concrete
Metal ties	Release agent
Scrap spacers	Vegetable oil
Sledgehammer	3½" deck screws

A visit from the concrete truck is definitely in order when you are pouring foundation walls. Larger trucks can deliver up to 10 cubic yards per load, so be sure you're ready to go when the delivery is scheduled.

Concrete Delivery

On all but the smallest foundation jobs, ordering a truck delivery of concrete is the most efficient and economical option for filling your forms. Correctly ordering just what you need will save time, money, and frustration. The best way to do this is to let the concrete provider do the math. Measure the length, width, and depth of all your forms and give this information to the sales desk operator. Make sure they know what you'll be using the concrete for. They'll be glad to design a mixture that's perfect for your situation.

As the customer, your biggest responsibility is to make certain that the forms are ready at delivery time, and that there is a clear path for getting the concrete to the jobsite.

On the job site, the truck feeds the concrete down a chute, with a maximum chute length of about 16 feet. Keep in mind that if the chute can't reach, or if the truck can't access the site (trucks are larger than most people imagine: about 35 feet long, 9 feet wide, and 14 feet tall, and weigh close to 80,000 pounds full), you'll need a pump. The truck will then feed the pump, which will feed the concrete under pressure through a hose to the site. A pumping rig adds a great deal of cost, so it's best to try to find an access route for the truck if at all possible. *Note: For many concrete projects you can deliver material from the truck chute to the forms in wheelbarrows, but the forms for foundation walls are almost always too high for this.*

Wall Form Construction ▶

A wall form is built with two framed sides (much like a standard 2 × 4 stud wall) covered with ¾" plywood. The two sides are joined together at each end by means of a stop board, which also shapes the end of the finished wall. The form is braced and staked in position.

Tie wires prevent the sides of the form from spreading under the force of the concrete. Temporary spacers maintain proper spacing between the sides while the form is empty; these are pulled out once the concrete is placed.

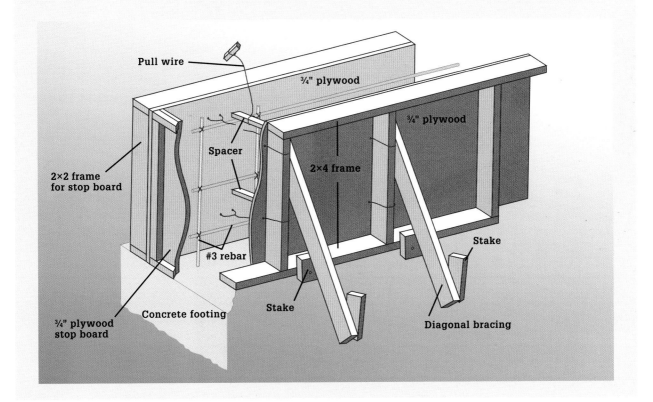

Pull wire
¾" plywood
¾" plywood
2×2 frame for stop board
Spacer
2×4 frame
#3 rebar
Stake
Concrete footing
Stake
Diagonal bracing
¾" plywood stop board

How to Build a Wall Form

Cut the plywood form boards to the desired height and attach 2 × 4 form braces on-edge to the sheets at 24" intervals. Or, if you're pouring a tall wall, every 16". The main purpose of these braces it to stiffen the plywood so it won't bow. Drive 3½" deck screws through the 2 × 4 and into the plywood, overdriving the screws so the heads are recessed ½". This will give the screws enough purchase to hold the braces in place. When building forms, always try to keep the screwheads on the outside of the forms so they can be removed.

2 × 4 brace

Support wire hole

Attach horizontal 2 × 4 braces to the vertical braces using deck screws driven toenail style, and then drill holes for the supporting wire ties on each side of each vertical brace at the point where it is intersected by a horizontal brace.

Cut 2 × 4 spreader inserts to the planned thickness of the wall. Slip them into position inside the form near the top, and tie some wire to them so they can be removed easily during the pour when the concrete reaches their level.

Position the forms in exact place on top of the footings. Where form assemblies butt together, attach a 2 × 4 or 2 × 6 vertical gusset at the seam. Tie into the existing foundation by wiring vertical rebar to the rebar pins you've anchored in the existing wall (see page 75).

Brace each form as you go with 2 × 4 braces and stakes, checking for level. Adjust as necessary. Continue to install rebar horizontally as you add forms. Tie the rebar lengths together with tie wire, overlapping the ends by at least 12".

Fill the forms with concrete. Coat the inside of the forms with release oil, and begin pouring. If you are filling the forms from a wheelbarrow, fill up whole sections at once; if you are having the concrete placed directly from the truck, add a couple of feet at a time all the way around the perimeter so all forms are filled more or less at the same time.

Work the concrete with a square-end spade to help it settle and fill the form. Once the pour is done, hammer the sides or use a special vibrator called a stinger to further settle the material in the form, eliminating voids.

Strike off the concrete at the top of the foundation walls with a 2 × 4 or metal screed, moving the tool back and forth in sawing motion. Once the top surface is smooth and flush with the form tops all the way around, insert J-bolts for the mudsills of the addition. Space the J-bolts 4 ft. apart and 1 ft. from any connection or corner. Cover the concrete with sheet plastic and let it dry for several days before removing the forms.

Cutting through a hardened concrete foundation to install openings or run mechanical services is a major undertaking that can be avoided with a little planning. Fortunately, some simple techniques will allow you to accommodate a window or vent in a poured foundation wall, or run pipes or wiring underneath a slab.

Creating an opening in a concrete wall, whether it is a basement window or a pipe that needs to run through the perimeter wall of a crawlspace, is just a matter of securing a customized "blockout" in place in the form. The blockout materials must be as strong as the rest of the form so that they won't give way during the pour. Securely fastened in place, the right blockouts will create a cavity in whatever shape you need. For a pipe or wiring, simply drill a hole in the center of the intended pass-through and use a jigsaw to cut an opening equal in diameter to a piece of PVC pipe that has a slightly larger inside dimension than the outside dimension of the pipe you'll be running. PVC pipe also can be used as a conduit for wiring or cabling. Create custom pockets for other shapes using a form within a form.

Construct the outside dimensions in wood and securely screw it into place in the form. Make sure that the blockout will not be completely encapsulated by concrete.

Running pipes, ductwork, or wiring under a slab requires good preparation and proactive troubleshooting. First, it's wise to limit any direct contact between metal pipes or wiring and the concrete slab itself. Over time, the concrete will leach corrosive compounds that can eat into metal, causing wiring, water, or sewer lines to fail. You should also try to limit the number of plumbing connections made under the slab. Leaks are more likely to occur at connections, so the fewer there are, the fewer potential problem areas you'll have.

It's also a good idea to measure very carefully when laying out connections, such as a toilet flange, that come up through the slab. Any mistakes will be nearly impossible to re-route without cutting out part of the slab. In the final analysis, it's always best to run connections through the walls above the slab rather than trapped in the concrete.

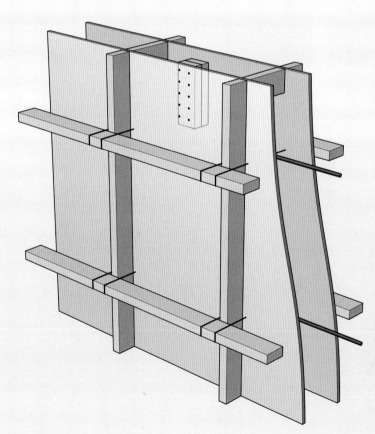

Create a pocket for a beam by using a solid block of wood built up from 2 × 4s or 2 × 6s cut and screwed together. Fix it to the inner side of the form, flush with the top of the form.

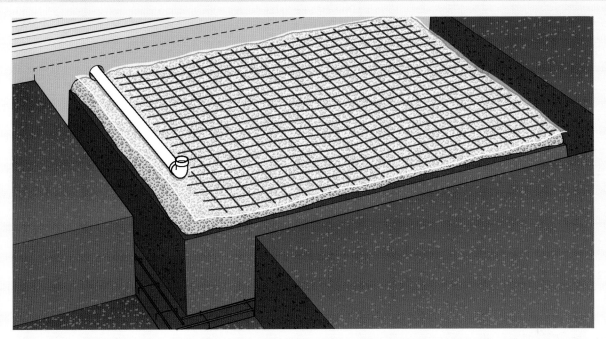

Set piping in place under a slab before pouring begins, but measure after installing the piping to double-check that the positioning is correct.

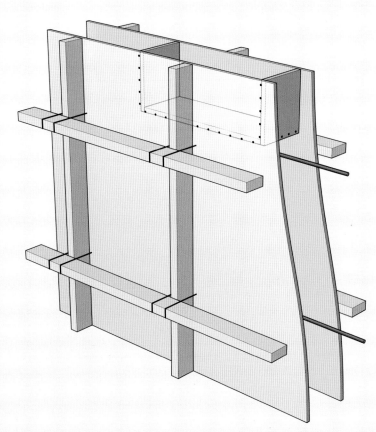

Build a blockout for a window by forming a "U" of the same plywood that you used in the form. Position it and check level and plumb, and screw it securely into place.

Waterproofing Foundation Walls

Water is the enemy of every foundation. If not directed away, it can undercut the foundation's base, causing a host of problems and ultimately even compromising the foundation's stability. Water needs only the tiniest of openings—a hairline crack in a concrete block mortar joint will do—to infiltrate a basement or crawl space and start creating the damp conditions that can result in mold and wood rot. But if water is the enemy, proper drainage and waterproofing are the weapons that can defeat it.

Waterproof coatings are the first step in protecting foundation walls from moisture. Among the many products available, the simplest are rubber-based coatings that are sprayed or rolled on, or stiffer asphalt-based compounds that are troweled onto the surface. These are relatively inexpensive and easy to use, but it can be difficult to apply them evenly. Where they are applied too thinly, they may break down over time. They also may require that the wall be prepped before application, because the compounds themselves usually won't fill holes such as those left by form ties.

Sheet membranes are a somewhat more expensive option. These have a strong adhesive on one side that ensures the membrane sticks securely to the concrete. But the adhesive makes working with the material a bit of a challenge. Membranes do, however, cover holes and imperfections, and can be quickly patched where they rip or bubble.

Bentonite panels—stiff boards impregnated with a type of absorbent clay—are a popular option among professionals. Once installed, the panels absorb water, swell, and consequently seal against infiltration. The drawback to Bentonite is that the material is not activated until it is exposed to the water in the soil—at which point you can't inspect the panels for full coverage.

Bituminous sealcoating is applied to a freshly stacked concrete block foundation wall prior to backfilling.

Regardless of which option you choose, waterproofing foundation walls is only half the battle. You also need to move standing water away from the foundation. This is done with a basic drainage system. A perforated pipe is laid in a gravel bed at the base of the foundation while it is exposed. Special drainage fabric is laid around the gravel to prevent infiltration of small soil particles, and the gravel is then covered with backfill and sod that is sloped away from the foundation. Rainwater seeps down through the soil and into the pipe, which carries it away from the foundation to a drain, open porous area such as a lawn, or—in large flat yards—a dry well.

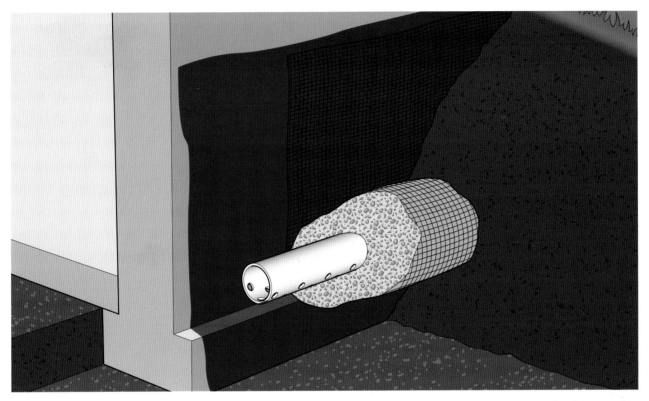

Effective foundation drainage is a layered system completely designed to direct water away from the foundation, from creating the proper grade slope at the top, to installing the perforated drainage pipe at the bottom.

Basement Drainage ▸

If you're building a basement foundation in an area with a high water table or where flooding is a concern, it's a good idea to install a sump pump system when you lay the basement slab. The system begins with a central drain in the middle of the slab, which is routed to a sump pump positioned in a small well laid at the same time as the slab. The pump pushes water from the drain up and out, ensuring that there is never standing water inside the basement. Although installing a sump pump system requires a lot more effort than simply laying a basement slab, putting one in before you finish the basement is a lot easier than retrofitting a finished basement.

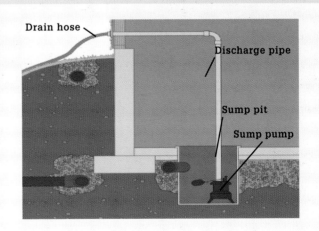

Insulating Foundations

Insulating the inside or outside of a foundation is an easy and simple improvement that can make for a much more comfortable and energy-efficient addition. In many areas of the country, insulation is required on the foundation walls that border heated space. Insulating the interiors of these walls can be easily done any time after the foundation walls are finished and before the floor structure is built.

There are many different ways and materials you can use to insulate your foundation. One of the most effective and easiest solutions is to use foam insulation board. Rigid foam board insulation is less susceptible than other types to insect infestation and will not hold moisture the way batting insulation can. The foam board is coated with building adhesive and installed on top of whatever waterproofing layer was applied to the foundation wall. The boards are butted to one another and the seams are sealed with house wrap seam tape.

You can also use foam board on the inside of crawl spaces. On the interior side of the foundation wall, a vapor barrier may be run first over the ground and then all the way up to the mudsill. The foam board insulation is installed over the vapor barrier just as it would be on the outside of the foundation. If the crawl space won't be subjected to a great deal of moisture, you can run fiberglass batting down the wall and over the ground vapor barrier, stapling the top edge to the mudsill. Weight down the bottom end with bricks or dirt.

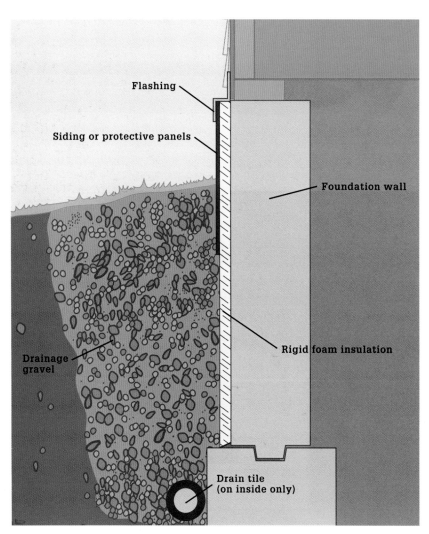

Apron insulation provided by rigid foam boards is an easy and effective way to enhance comfort in your basement without causing any major moisture issues.

Flashing

Siding or protective panels

Foundation wall

Rigid foam insulation

Drainage gravel

Drain tile (on inside only)

Insulating concrete forms are made of rigid foam insulation boards and they are meant to be left in place to provide insulation after the concrete walls dry.

Insulating Concrete Forms (ICF) ▶

Combining the convenience of a prefabricated form with the efficiency of a customized layer of insulation, Insulating Concrete Forms (ICF) are a well-established product among professional builders, but now they are becoming popular with homeowners as well. ICFs are constructed of high-density plastic foam that is intended to remain in place after the concrete sets. Different manufacturers offer different systems, ranging from interlocking blocks to full-size panels. Regardless of the connection system, all are designed to be easily constructed on site with a minimum of time, effort, and expertise.

- **R-Value.** The insulation performance of ICF foundations far exceeds fiberglass-insulated walls, making the entire space more energy efficient. This is especially important when the basement foundation abuts living space.
- **Construction time.** Because ICFs are preformed, setup is streamlined and the forms are much quicker to set up than traditional forms would be. And because ICFs stay in place permanently, there's no break-down stage. Just let the concrete cure 5 to 7 days, and you're ready to build on the forms.
- **Durability.** ICFs can withstand the same stresses and strains that a poured concrete foundation can. They

are reinforced with rebar in much the same way as a traditional poured foundation is, and the insulation actually helps the concrete cure and set up properly.
- **Green building practice.** ICFs greatly reduce the construction waste created by building, breaking down, and discarding forms. In addition, the expanded or extruded polystyrene used in forming ICFs does not off-gas or break down the way some other types of insulation do.

The challenges in using ICFs relate largely to cost and inexperience with the technology. The initial cost is usually higher than with other types of forms, but energy cost savings can make up the difference over the long run. Check with your local building department to make sure ICFs are code compliant in your area. Although not difficult to set up, the ICFs must be installed in accordance with the manufacturer's instructions. For instance, running some mechanical services can require cutting into the plastic foam surface; if done improperly, this can compromise the insulating value of the section. This becomes more of an issue if you hope to finish the basement space and will want to hang a wall surface on the interior of the ICF. ICF manufacturers offer guidance for most construction situations.

Framing the Floor

The floor structure is the stage for the rest of your addition, so take pains to maintain a level surface and solid construction throughout. You'll also make all the construction that follows that much easier, from framing the walls to laying down the final flooring.

Because so much depends on the floor structure, precise measurements are vital. Before you even start framing the floor, re-check level and plumb on the foundation walls and re-measure the existing floor structure. You can adjust to suit minor variations by shimming the mudsill where necessary.

Once you begin building the floor, constantly check level and measurements, and always use sound construction techniques. For instance, never butt floor joists up to one another where the ends meet over a beam. They should overlap to ensure the strongest possible floor structure. And to prevent squeaky floors and add to the integrity, brace with metal X-braces or solid wood blocking between joists even if the codes don't require it for your addition.

Otherwise, you need only follow the plans. If your building plans have been carefully developed, they address code considerations and best standards and practices. Put all the pieces in place accurately and the structural load will be evenly distributed across the floor's surface, guaranteeing a floor that won't sag over time and that provides a comfortable, solid feel underfoot.

Tools & Materials ▸

Hammer	Metal joist hangers
Circular saw	16d nails
Lag screws	10d nails
2 × 6s (pressure-treated and not)	¾" tongue-and-groove plywood sheets

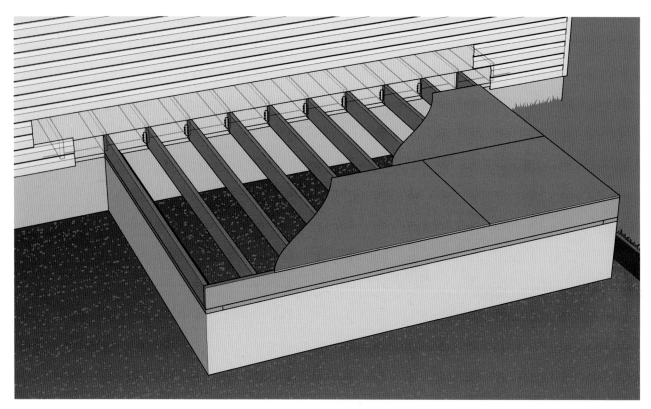

The floor structure for a new addition is not complicated, but making sure it is built correctly and carefully is extremely important.

How to Frame a Floor

Attach 2 × 6 pressure-treated mudsills to the tops of the foundation walls. They must be positioned flush with the outside edges of the foundation wall. Lay the sills in position so the J-bolts set in the foundation walls mark drilling points in the underside of the sill plates. Drill guide holes for the bolts. Secure the mudsills with the bolts and washers and nuts. *Tip: Add a layer of sill-seal barrier between the sill and the foundation wall.*

Cut the rim joists to length and then toenail them to the mudsill. Align the outside face of each rim joist with the outer edges of the sill plate. Mark the inside face of the mudsill for the joist positions. Use galvanized nails whenever nailing into treated wood.

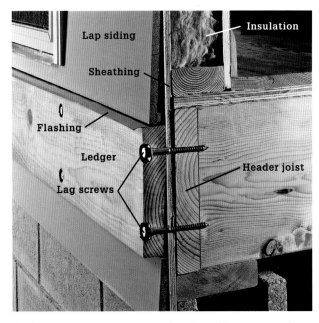

Nail metal joist hangers to the home's existing rim joist, to support the new joists. In most areas, the joists do not need to be made from pressure treated lumber, but if they do you'll need to use triple-coated, hot-dipped fasteners. Position the hangers 16" on center, unless otherwise designated by code. Remove siding and sheathing as needed to expose the rim joist in the rim joist area.

Option: In some areas, you may be allowed to remove only the siding and attach a ledger board instead of attaching hangers directly to the house's rim joist.

(continued)

4

Cut the floor joists to length and set the ends in the hangers, with the other ends resting on the mudsill, flush against the new rim joist. Crown all joists (the bow facing upwards, not sagging down). Secure the joists in the hangers with joist hanger nails or 10d common nails, filling every predrilled nail hole in each hanger. Nail the joists into the hangers and nail the opposite ends to the new rim joist. Check joists for level.

Option: If the subfloor sheets you are installing do not have tongue-and-groove edges, or if you'll need to cut it such that two pieces will meet at a plain butt joint, install blocking to support any seams that will not fall over joists. Blocking also helps stiffen the floor. Use three 16d common nails to attach the end of each piece of blocking to the joists.

5

Install the subfloor sheeting. If you are using sheathing that has no tongue-and-groove edges, install the subfloor so there is a ⅛" expansion gap between panels. Apply a bead of construction adhesive to the tops of the joists before setting each panel. If you have installed nailing blocks, make sure panel seams fall over blocks.

Tongue-and-Groove Sheathing ▶

Subfloor panels must be made of sheathing that is rated for use in a floor system. These may be made either of plywood or oriented-strand boards. They are generally ¾" thick (or within a ¹⁄₁₆" or ¹⁄₃₂" of ¾"). Subfloor sheathing often is milled with tongue-and-groove edges that fit together during installation. This provides greater rigidity and reduces bounce. In some cases, using tongue-and-groove sheathing panels can eliminate the need to install nailers between joists if a seam will fall over the spot.

Engineered Lumber ▸

Engineered lumber offers a viable alternative to the dimensional sawn lumber used in the structural members of your floor system. Engineered members, such as beams and truss chords, are constructed from a variety of wood fiber sources—reclaimed wood, mill waste, etc.—that are bonded and manufactured into lumber that performs the same job as their sawn counterparts, only more efficiently. Because engineered lumber uses byproducts that would otherwise have gone into the waste stream, this type of lumber is considered a "green" building option. Engineered components are usually more expensive than sawn pieces, but are lighter and easier to work with. Engineered beams can bear greater amounts of weight than dimensional lumber of the same size, which can sometimes allow you to fit a structural element into a spot that would otherwise be too small.

Two key pieces that can be used in constructing an addition floor are engineered "I" joists or beams, and truss joists.

Engineered I beams come in the same sizes as standard lumber but in the I-form common to steel beams. Light and strong, an entire joist can be carried by a single worker. However, because of their composition, I joists and beams tend to be somewhat "floppy" over their lengths, and are consequently cross-braced more frequently than sawn joists are.

Truss joists are fabricated components with an open-web design similar to the steel joists and beams seen on many bridges. Wooden truss joists are usually constructed of pieces of smaller lumber, such as 2 × 4s. The web design gives the joists exceptional strength and offers more room to run plumbing, wiring and other services through the joists.

Special hangers and braces may be required for engineered lumber, but otherwise the installation process is the same.

Proper floor support is crucial to not only guarantee that the addition's floor doesn't sag or flex, but also to provide necessary structural stability to the whole addition. Building codes and manufacturers instructions will mandate exactly how long you can run an engineered joist.

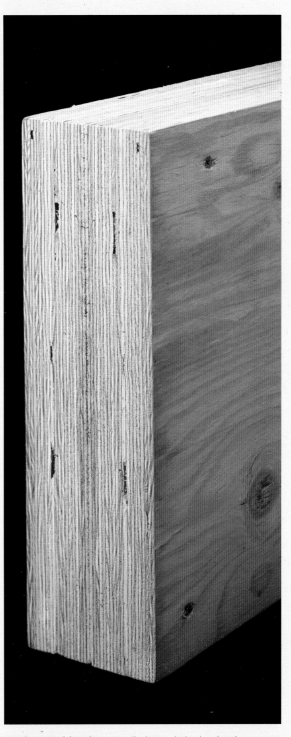

Engineered lumber usually is made by laminating plywood, OSB or sawn lumber into thick beams with widths corresponding to standard dimensional stock. This beam is made from face-glued strips of plywood and it can span greater distances than a beam of the same width made from solid 2× stock

BUILDING
A ROOM ADDITION

Additions
& Bumpouts

Adding a completely new space onto your home is one way of putting your own stamp on the structure and re-defining your house in a manner that suits your tastes and the way you'd like to live. Unlike a conversion that simply alters an existing room or space, a new room addition or even a more modest "bumpout" allows you to create something completely new and unique.

When building an expansion or bumpout, you are free to control the dimensions, lighting, exterior look, and practically every other aspect of the project (provided you remain in compliance with local codes and ordinances, of course). You can choose whether to add a grandiose entrance hall with an open sitting room for entertaining, or to keep the whole affair more low key with a doubling of the square footage in a back bedroom that may be unseen from the curb.

In this chapter:

- Choosing a Bumpout or Room Addition
- Framing a Wall
- Constructing the Addition's Roof
- Installing Asphalt Shingles
- Sheathing Exterior Walls
- Building Wrap
- Installing Siding
- Soffits, Fascia & Gutters
- Installing Windows
- Installing an Entry Door
- Wiring an Addition
- Circuits for a Room Addition
- Plumbing the Addition
- Heating and Cooling an Addition
- Insulating the Addition
- Finishing the Interior
- Installing Casing
- Choosing Floorcoverings

Choosing a Bumpout or Room Addition

The choice between a smaller, simpler bumpout and a full-scale room addition is driven by the amount of space you need or want, the function the new space will serve, and the practical restrictions of budget, codes, and property lines. It's a choice that may come down to commitment: if you think you'll eventually be trading up and only need a little more space, the bumpout may be the way to go. If you love your home and don't see yourself ever leaving it, and want to add a luxurious new element, the room addition may well make more sense.

A bumpout is the more modest of the two. Generally, bumpouts simply increase the space in an existing room. The beauty of a bumpout is that you can add significant extra space with a more moderate budget and less work than a full room addition would require. The restrained nature of this type of addition means that they are usually planned to avoid running new mechanical services. The construction itself is also less in-depth. Depending on the type of bumpout you select and where it's located, you may be able to use a fairly simple foundation, such as a post-and-pier or slab-on-grade. Many bumpouts use a simpler shed roof rather than building a peaked style. The fact is, although some bumpout projects add to the look of the house (such as a bay window), in most cases the bumpout is all about the extra interior area.

A modest bumpout on the side of this cottage-style house added space for a dedicated eating area off of a smallish kitchen.

In contrast, a room addition is, in many ways, it's own structure. Where you'd likely choose a bumpout to provide extra seating, open space, and windows in a kitchen, a full addition would be the choice if the space will encompass more than a single room, as with a master bedroom suite. It also focuses on function as well as adding space. Special fixtures and services may be included in an addition if it is to serve as a special-purpose room, such as a home theater or master bath. A room addition will have a major impact on how both the house and the property are perceived inside and out.

Differences aside, a bumpout and a full room addition are built using the same construction techniques, and both rely on sound framing and finish work to integrate fluidly with the rest of the home. So the decision ultimately comes down to balancing how much the new space will improve life in your home versus the value it adds and the cost it incurs.

A full room addition provides one or more new living spaces that increase the total square footage of your house. They can be added just about anywhere you can fit one in. This second story addition adds a spacious new bedroom to this house, at the same time creating a sheltered entry area below.

Bumpouts vs. Room Additions ▸

The term bumpout, as it applies to remodeling, is fairly nonspecific and casual. Typically, a bumpout is understood to be small, framed projection of one room wall outward to expand interior space. Because the bumpout requires a roof and a foundation, it would technically count as an addition, even though it is not adding a full room. Bumpouts where HVAC systems or plumbing are not extended can be relatively cheap to build, although if you are calculating costs on a per-square-foot basis, the fact that it has a smaller footage amount by which you divide the total costs often means bumpouts cost more.

The Modular Option ▸

Over a century ago, a group of builders decided that constructing a home outdoors was not the most efficient construction method. They determined that using the same construction methods in the more predictable environment of a factory, combined with the standardized techniques of assembly-line production, could produce a more consistently standardized structure. And that's how they came to develop the first pre-fabricated homes.

Today's modular builders work from the same basic idea: Building the components for a home in the climate-controlled environment of a factory and exploiting economies of scale translates to lower overall costs, quicker production times, and a generally more efficient building process with less construction waste. Traditional builders will tout the quality and customization of a stick-built addition constructed on site, but there's no denying that there are many compelling reasons to consider prefabricated options.

Although you can buy prefabricated panels and constructed sections, the most popular choices for prefabricated room additions are modular units, or "modules." Modular manufacturers create entire rooms that are transported whole and connected to the existing house on site.

Modular rooms are offered as either second-story additions that drop right in place once the existing roof is removed, or room additions that can be either detached as standalone structures, or integrated rooms designed to be tied to a wall of the house. The modules themselves are offered in a wide range of configurations and sizes, limited mostly by the fact that they are delivered over the highway and subject to width restrictions. However, individual modules can be combined to create, for instance, a bedroom suite.

Manufacturers offer a growing array of customization options, but upscale versions are where the cost gaps between modular and traditional stick construction narrow. Many modular manufacturers can also meet contemporary "green" standards and some even offer construction conforming to demanding LEED (Land Environment Economics and Development) standards.

Even if you choose modular for your room addition, you'll likely need professional help in preparing the site and installing foundation, as well as running utilities and ensuring the entire job is up to code. Incorporating a modular addition is not really a do-it-yourself project, but it can be a money-saving—and certainly a time-saving—option.

Before

After

Framing a Wall

Measurements are critical in framing a wall, but the actual components that go into the structure are fairly basic. Refer to your plans and be sure to account for all of the elements of your framed wall, including door and window openings. For any frame carpentry it usually works best to build the wall on the ground or floor, including the sill and cap plates. Then, raise the assembly, position it, and anchor it to the structural members beneath the subfloor.

Tools & Materials ▸

Hammer   Carpenter's pencil
Tape measure   2 × 6 lumber
Level   16d nails
Circular saw

Hand Nailing ▸

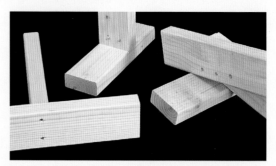

The best hand-nailing technique for joining framing members depends on whether you assemble the framed wall and then raise it, or you add boards one at a time in their final position. If you're assembling the wall on the floor or ground, end-nail the studs to the plates whenever you can (left sample). End-nailed joints, usually made with 10d common nails, are strong and fast to make. To double up wall studs or headers, facenail the parts (right sample) with 8d common nails. Facenailing is also used for attaching jack studs to king studs. To fasten a vertical stud to a top or sole plate that is already in place, toenailing (middle sample) is your best option.

The wall raising is one of the more exciting moments in construction, as the shape of the structure begins to emerge. The basic idea is to build the addition as completely as you can before you cut into the house.

How to Frame a Wall

Sight down the studs and top and sole plates and replace any with warps or obvious imperfections. Cut the plates and studs to uniform lengths, using a stop block. If you have designed your addition with 8-ft.-tall walls, look for pre-cut 92⅝" studs. *Note: In most climates today, your wall framing members should be made of 2 × 6 lumber, not the 2 × 4 lumber seen here. Code requirements for minimum wall insulation generally require a deeper 2 × 6 stud bay.*

Gang-mark the wall stud locations on the sole and top plates. Cut the plates to length first and clamp the ends together, making sure they are flush. In most cases, the studs should be 16" on-center. Draw an X on the side of the marking lines where the stud will fit.

With sole plate lying on-edge, face nail through the sole plate and into the bottoms of the studs. Use two or three 16d common nails per stud. Then, nail the top plate to the other end of the studs so that the wall is framed, lying down.

Build the wall corners. There are several ways you can create interlocking corners so the wall can be attached easily and accurately to the adjoining framed wall. Here, a pair of studs are installed perpendicular to the corner stud to create nailing surfaces for the adjoining wall and for the exterior wall sheathing at the corner.

(continued)

5

Measure the diagonals of the wall to check that it is square. If the diagonal measurements are not identical, use pressure (and clamps if necessary) to pull the wall frame into square. If the diagonals just won't match, measure the wall studs and make sure none of the studs is too long or too short.

6

Raise the first wall. Nail guide blocks to the outside edge of the rim joist to create stops for the soleplate. With a helper, raise the wall into position and check the studs for plumb and the wall for level. If the wall abuts the house make sure it fits cleanly against the wall (the siding should have been removed at the wall tie-in spot by this point).

7

Nail the soleplate to the structural members beneath the subfloor with pairs of 16d common nails spaced every 14" to 16". Attach a 2 × 4 brace to an intermediate stud and anchor the other end to a stake in the ground.

8

Plumb the wall, then nail the corner wall stud to the existing house structure. If you did not plan your addition so the wall meets the house at a house stud location, you'll need to remove the exterior wall sheathing in the installation area and install 2 × 4 or 2 × 6 nailing blocks between the wall studs on each side of the opening.

9

Begin building the second wall. If the wall includes an exterior door, nail king studs into place allowing for the rough-in width of the pre-hung door unit plus 3" (for the jack studs). Face nail jack studs in place.

Constructing a Header ▸

Door and window openings are wider than normal stud spacing, so they require a head beam, or header, to transfer the overhead weight to the studs at the sides of the opening. Professional builders commonly make their own headers by sandwiching ½" plywood between two 2× pieces. The width of the 2× depends on the width of the opening and how much overhead load the wall carries; check your local codes. The pieces are laminated with construction adhesive and then nailed from both sides to create a strong header that measures exactly as wide as the thickness of a 2 × 4 wall. For 2 × 6 walls, construct a box from parallel 2×s on all sides and fill it with insulation.

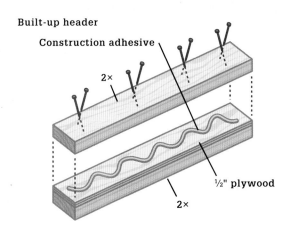

Built-up header

Construction adhesive

2×

½" plywood

2×

(continued)

Place the header on the tops of the jack studs with the ends flush against the king studs. Drive 10d common nails through the king studs and into the header. Then, cut cripple studs to fit between the header and the top plate, maintaining the 16" o.c. spacing. Toe-nail the cripple studs into position.

Add extra blocking next to the door opening for improved security.

Jack stud

Window sill

Add framing for windows as needed. Nail king studs into place, allowing for the rough-in width of the window plus 3". Face nail jack studs into place above the sole plate to the bottom of the sill.

Nail a doubled 2 × 4 window sill into place on top of jack studs. Drive 10d common nails through the king studs and into the ends of the double sill.

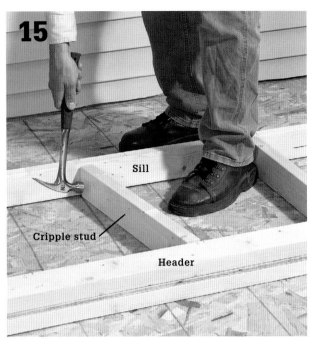

Nail the window header into position above the top jack studs, face-nailing it through the king studs.

Nail cripple studs above the header and below the sill, adding more cripples as necessary to maintain at least 16" o.c. spacing for studs.

Tie adjoining wall frames together by nailing them at the corners, and add overlapping top plates to lock the walls together.

Constructing the Addition's Roof

A well-built roof helps define architectural style while protecting your house from the elements. An addition's roof is no different—it too has to complement the architecture and shield the space below. But the roof on an addition must also link the new space to the existing structure, both visually and structurally.

The first step in effectively making that link is choosing a roof style. Although a basic triangular gable roof is the most common—and one of the easiest to frame—the look or function of your particular addition may be better suited to a more complex hip roof with intersecting planes and multiple valleys, an easy-to-build shed roof with its single sloping plane, or the distinctive gambrel roof that adds two additional angles to the gable's design and increases the attic's head room.

The possibilities increase when you consider the many variations of these basic styles, but the roof you choose for your addition will likely be most influenced by the existing architecture. Because any new roof must complement and tie into existing roof lines, a good design normally matches the addition's roof to the style used on the rest of the house. That's the easiest way to prevent the addition from looking like an afterthought.

Practical considerations also play a big role in roof choice. The most important of these is the angle of the roof's slope, called the pitch. The appropriate pitch for your roof depends on a number of variables, such as rafter size and spacing and local climate conditions. For instance, a more severe pitch is better where heavy snowfall is common but a more moderate pitch will

resist high winds better. Pitch is expressed as the "rise" or vertical height in relation to the "run" or span of the roof surface. For instance, a common pitch would be 6-in-12, meaning that the roof slopes 6 inches for every 12 inches of span. Other variables include the depth of the eaves, the soffit style, and end wall overhang, if any. Because your original roof was engineered with these variables in mind, the easiest and most common strategy is to mimic the existing roof and features.

Regardless, the roof details will be worked out in the planning stage and will be detailed in the building plans, according to best practices and code requirements. The plans serve as a roadmap for framing the roof, a process that requires a well-thought-out construction process because it happens mostly in midair. Because the framing members of a roof are usually large and unwieldy, it's unwise to attempt framing even a small roof without at least one or two strong helpers.

Tools & Materials ▸

Carpenter's square	Metal rafter ties
Hammer	16d and 8d nails
Tape measure	2 × 10 ridge board
Carpenter's pencil	2 × 6 joists
Jigsaw	2 × 4s (for ties
Table saw	and blocking)
Circular saw	

Roof rafters are usually attached to the wall top plates with a combination of fasteners and metal hangers or ties.

Cutting the Template Rafter

Framing the roof will go much quicker if you measure, mark, and cut one rafter, and then use that rafter as a template for laying out the other rafters. All rafters will have top and bottom plumb cuts that are parallel to the roof ridge board, as well as bird's mouth cuts that create an angled notch that fits over the cap plate of the framed wall. Depending on the soffit structure of your roof, you may or may not need a decorative tail cut. The rafter shown here is cut for a 6-in-12 roof pitch.

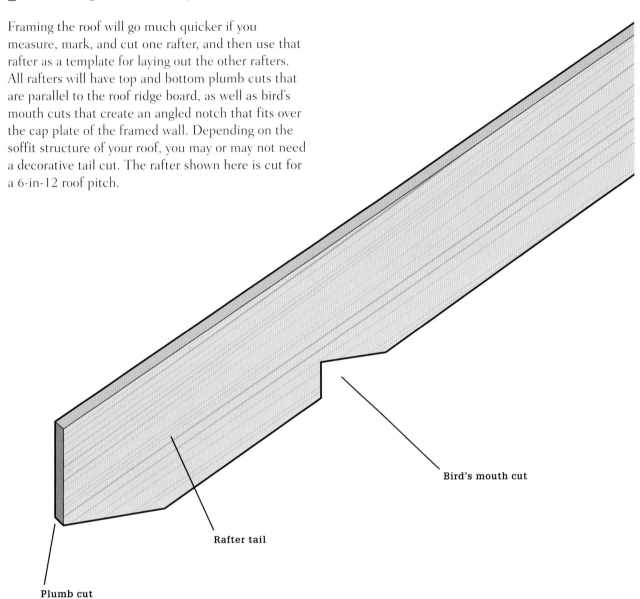

Bird's mouth cut

Rafter tail

Plumb cut

The two cuts you'll need to make on any rafter are the plumb cuts, which cause the ends of the rafter to be vertical when installed, and the bird's mouth cut, which creates a notch for the rafter to fit over the wall. Some rafter ends also receive a decorative tail cut.

Rafter Ties ▸

For added strength (or as required by code), use metal fasteners or braces to attach the rafters. Always use hardware rated for the size rafters you are using and fasten them securely in place using the recommended fasteners. If you live in a hurricane or earthquake zone, your local codes will have very specific rafter tie requirements that you will need to follow.

How to Cut a Template Rafter

Mark the top plumb cut where the rafter will fit against the ridge board. *Tip: Sight down the rafter to determine which edge, if either, crowns. When installing the rafter, you'll want to position the board with the crown facing in a frown-like orientation—the crown holds up the weight of the roof better.*

Measure and mark the overall length of the rafter, and then mark the bottom plumb cut so it is parallel to, and the same angle as, the top plumb cut.

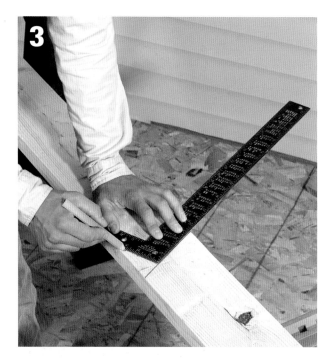

Mark the bird's mouth cut. Measure from top to the outside edge of wall, and mark the bird's mouth plumb cut in from that point. Use the framing square to square and mark off the level cut.

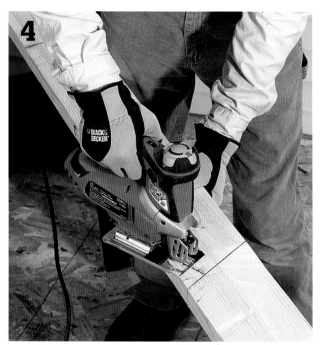

Make the cuts. Use a circular saw to make the plumb cuts and a jigsaw to make the bird's mouth cuts, and then test fit the template rafter. Once it fits perfectly, label it as the template and use it to mark the rest of the rafters.

How to Frame a Roof

Mark the positions of the rafters and ceiling joists onto the top plates of the framed walls. Rafters should sit above wall stud location, if possible.

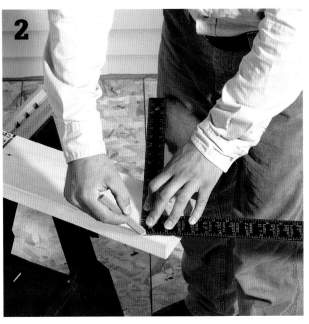

Mark and cut the ends of joists as necessary to match rafter width and roof slope. Mark the first joist in place, then copy the cuts on the remaining rafters.

Toenail the rim joists to the top of the wall and reinforce the connections with metal ties. The ends of the rim joists should be flush with the edges of the front wall and the outer faces should be set back 1½" to create a recess for the vertical rafter supports.

Adjustable Ridge Board Supports ▸

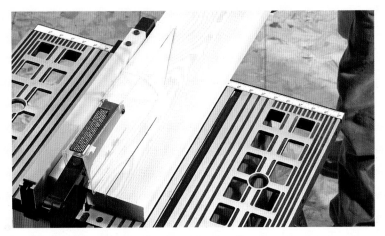

One of the challenges of framing a roof is dealing with large, heavy, and cumbersome framing members. The heaviest is usually the ridge board, which ideally should be in place for the rafters to be installed accurately. But because the ridge board can't simply float in space, it needs to be supported while the rafters are being positioned and attached. Simple 2 × 8 supports nailed to the joist and ridge board can hold the ridge in place with very little flex in the ridge board positioning. To make this "fork" brace, use a table saw to cut the shoulders of a notch centered along one end and running down the length of the brace. The notch should be slightly wider than the thickness of the ridge board. Each ridge board brace should be about 10" to 12" longer than the required height of the ridge from the top plate.

(continued)

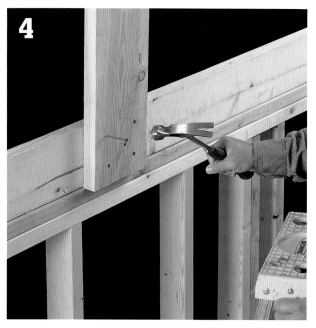

Build a pair of temporary ridge board supports to hold the ridge board in place. Cut a notch for the ridge board in the top of each support. The distance from the uncut end of the support to the bottom of the notch should be the planned distance between the tops of the walls and the bottom of the ridge board. Use at least four nails to face-nail the supports in place at both ends of the addition. Set the ridge board in position in the supports and tack in place. Install the ceiling joists by toenailing to the top plates of the walls and then reinforcing with metal ties.

Set a rafter in place against the house siding, making sure it fits cleanly against the ridge board and rests cleanly on the wall. On each side of the ridge, trace the top edges of the rafter onto the siding, then add 2" for sheathing, shingles, flashing, and (for vinyl roofs) J-channel to make cutting lines.

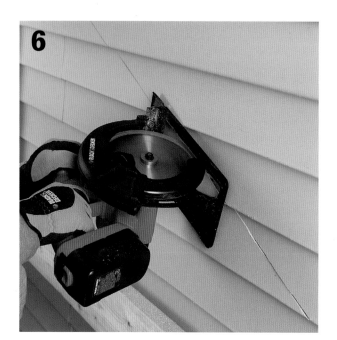

Cut out the siding to make space for the rafter against the wall. *Tip: To cut vinyl siding, reverse the blade direction on a circular saw or cordless trim saw. Once the siding is removed, find the stud locations with a stud finder and mark them.*

Mark, cut, and test fit the gable end rafters to ensure the accuracy of the template. Toenail the rafters to the wall plate and also facenail the rafters next to the house at stud locations.

8

Attach the rafters to the ridge board using hanger brackets. Make sure the distances between rafters are equal, which confirms that the rafters are parallel.

9

Install rafter ties near the tops of the rafters to stiffen the roof structure. Trim the top corners of the 2 × 4 ties first, to match the roof slope.

10

Install 2 × 4 nailers at the front of the roof gables at 16" intervals.

11

If your plans include a gable overhang, or "rake," nail lookouts between the gable-end rafter and the overhang rafter. The lookouts should be installed so their top edges are flush with the rafter tops and they should be cut from the same thickness of 2× stock as the rafters. If your plan includes a fascia, nail the fascia board (or the subfascia) to the rafter ends.

Variations: Tying Into a Perpendicular Roof

Positioning an addition at an angle to the existing structure can add interest to the architecture, and may be necessary to accommodate the confines of your property boundaries and setbacks. But tying an addition's roof into a perpendicular roof presents a more complex framing challenge than simply running the addition's roof parallel to the existing roof.

If you are adding a single-story room addition where the living space butts against your house and a gabled roof intersects your house roof at a perpendicular angle in the eave area, cutting into the old roof and adding the new structure is relatively simple, as seen on the next page. But a roof that penetrates higher up and adds living space below, as with a gable dormer, can be a bit trickier to frame (see pages 118–119). The intersection of the two roofs involves multiple angles that require jack rafters to be trimmed with compound cuts. The cuts themselves vary depending on the slope of the roof. The instructions in the demonstration project seen here apply to a roof with a 6-in-12 slope. But you can determine the necessary setback placement of the roof plates and the angles you'll need to use in making the jack rafter cuts by consulting a construction calculator, framing or speed square, or the tables available on many professional construction association websites. Obviously, this is complicated carpentry; be sure your skills are up to the task, or seek a professional carpenter's help for this part of the framing.

Tools & Materials ▸

Circular saw
Cordless drill
Tape measure
Chalk line
Level
Staple gun
2 × 10 ridge board
8d and 16d nails
Fall arrest harness
　and leash
¾" OSB sheets
Building paper
Ice guard membrane
　(as necessary)
Metal drip edge

Joining two roofs is considerably more complicated than simply extending a roofline or butting a new roof up against a wall.

Extending a Gable Roof

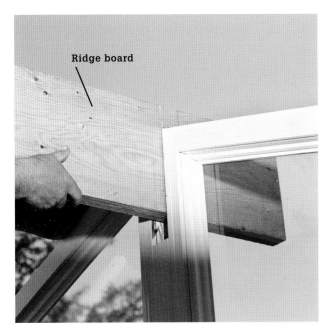

Ridge board

Build the structure to support the end of the ridge board opposite the new roof penetration and set the ridge board into rough position. Cutting the pole slightly long will allow you to make any length adjustments that you need.

Ridge board

Wall cap plate

Cut a small hole in the roof over the wall cap plate location. The hole needs to be at least large enough to accommodate three 2 × 6 supports that are laminated into a cradle for the ridge board. Level the ridge board over the hole and measure down to find the required height for the cradle to fit between the pole and the wall cap. Make the L-shaped cradle to this dimension and, with the ridge board removed, toenail the cradle to the plate.

Trim the end of the ridge board to fit flat on the sloped roof and set it onto the cradle. Secure the other end of the ridge board and then attach the pole to the cradle by face-screwing through the cradle upright.

Install the roof structure (here, structural insulated roof panels (SIPs) are connected directly to the top of the ridge board with pole barn screws). Use metal valley flashing to transition between the new roof and the old.

How to Add a Dormer-style Gable Roof

Support the new ridge board with braces at either end. Use a straightedge to mark the roof angle onto the ridge board face. Cut the end of the ridge board to fit the slope and cut the opposite end to length. When working on an asphalt-shingle roof be sure to wear soft-sole shoes. Fall-arresting gear is always a good idea, too.

Strip the shingles and underlayment in a triangular pattern, starting 1 ft. above the point where the ridge board will attach to the roof, and running all the way down to the roof edge.

Nail the ridge board in place. If there is a rafter under the sheathing at the attachment point, nail the ridge board directly to it. If not, nail blocking between two rafters in the attic, as a nailing surface for the house-end of the ridge board.

Snap a chalk line between the top edge of the ridge board and the point where the roofs will intersect at the eaves. Snap a second chalk line below the first, to account for the required setback according to the slope of the roof. In the case of the 6-in-12 slope of this roof, the setback is ¾".

Cut 2 × 6 plates to run between the ridge board and roof edge on both sides. Nail the roof plates into place along the inner chalk lines on both sides of the ridge board.

Measure and mark the rafter placement on the ridge board and roof plate. Once marked, measure the crown edge length for each rafter, from ridge board to roof plate. Also measure the compound angles where each end of each rafter will fall.

Cut the short rafters to length. Make the compound angle end cuts with a circular saw set to the appropriate bevel angle. You can also make these cuts on a compound miter saw.

Set each rafter into position and test the fit. Adjust as necessary so the ends make clean contact with both the ridge board and the roof plate. Attach the rafters by toenailing or use metal fasteners if required by code.

How to Install Roof Underlayment

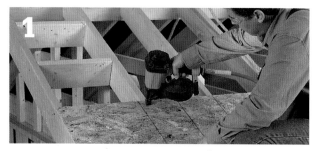

Nail a full sheet of oriented-strand board (OSB) or exterior-grade plywood rated sheathing to the rafter tops. Make sure the sheathing meets the minimum thickness requirements for your project. Follow the nailing schedules required by your local codes. Spacing of 6" on-center is common along the panel edges; 2½" × 8d galvanized box nails are typical when hand-nailing; 0.131" × 2½" clipped head or bent shank nails are used most often for pneumatic nailing. Start at the bottom, gable-end corner.

Start installing the second row of roof sheathing with a half sheet to stagger the joints. Leave a ⅛" gap between sheets to allow for expansion (unless you are using tongue-and-groove sheathing, where the expansion gap sets itself if the panels are installed correctly). *Tip: Tack the corners of the panel by handnailing and then, when the panel is safely in position, use a pneumatic nailer to fill in the field.*

Installing Drip Edge & Building Paper ▸

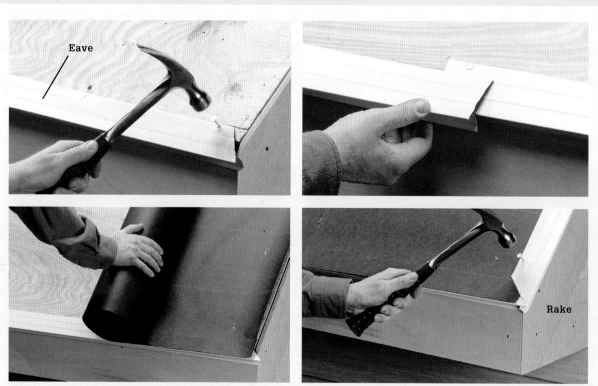

The metal drip edge flashing and the building paper are woven together during the installation to create a barrier that sheds water properly. It is important that you install drip edge and building paper in the correct order. First, cut a 45° miter at one end of the drip edge using aviation snips. Place the drip edge along the eaves end of the roof, aligning the mitered end with the rake edge. Nail the drip edge in place every 12". Overlap pieces of drip edge by 2". Install drip edge across the entire eaves, ending with a mitered cut on the opposite corner. Apply felt paper, and ice guard if needed, to the roof, overhanging the eaves by ⅜". Cut a 45° miter in a piece of drip edge and install it along the rake edge, forming a miter joint with the drip edge along the eaves. Overlap pieces by 2", making sure the higher piece is on top at the overlap. Apply drip edge all the way to the peak. Install drip edge along the other rake edges the same way.

Option: Install one or two courses of ice guard membrane at the eave area in colder climates and as required by local codes. This self-adhesive product forms a fully-bonded layer of protection to prevent ice dams from infiltrating beneath the roofcovering as snow melts.

Roll building paper horizontally and install drip edge flashing. Overlap the rows of paper at least 4".

Install building paper on one side of the roof up to the ridge, then cover the other side and overlap ridge by at least 4". Staple down the overlap with a hammer stapler.

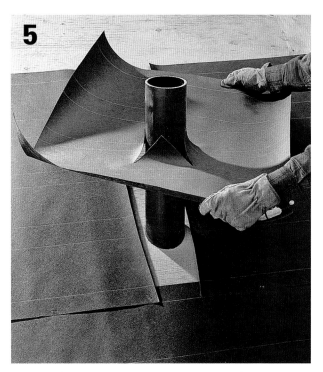

Make sure any obstructions or penetrations in the building paper layer are patched over with building paper or with ice guard membrane. You will still need to flash penetrations such as this vent pipe during the roofcovering installation.

Installing Asphalt Shingles

If you want to install asphalt shingles on your roof, then you're in good company. Asphalt shingles, also known as composition shingles, are the roofing of choice for nearly four out of five homeowners in America. They perform well in all types of climate, are available in a multitude of colors, shapes, and textures to complement every housing design, and are less expensive than most other roofing products.

Asphalt shingles are available as either fiberglass shingles or organic shingles. Both types are made with asphalt, the difference being that one uses a fiberglass reinforcing mat, while the other uses a cellulose-fiber mat. Fiberglass shingles are lighter, thinner, and have a better fire rating. Organic shingles have a higher tear strength, are more flexible in cold climates, and are used more often in northern regions.

Although the roofing market has exploded with innovative new asphalt shingle designs, such as the architectural or laminated shingle that offers a three-dimensional look, the standard three-tab asphalt

shingle is still the most common, which is the product we're using for this addition. The tabs provide an easy reference for aligning shingles for installation.

To help get the job done faster, rent an air compressor and pneumatic roofing gun. This will greatly reduce the time you spend nailing.

Tools & Materials ▸

Aviation snips	Caulk gun
Carpenter's square	Flashing
Chalk line	Shingles
Flat bar	Nailing cartridges
Roofer's hatchet or	Roofing cement
pneumatic nailer	Roofing nails
Utility knife	(⅞", 1¼")
Straightedge	Rubber gasket nails
Tape measure	

Stagger shingles for effective protection against leaks. If the tab slots are aligned in successive rows, water forms channels, increasing erosion of the mineral surface of the shingles. Creating a 6" offset between rows of shingles—with the three-tab shingles shown above—ensures that the tab slots do not align.

How to Install Three-tab Shingles

Cover the roof with felt paper (page 121) and install drip edge (page 120). Snap a chalk line onto the felt paper or ice guard 11½" up from the eaves edge to mark the alignment of the starter course. This will result in a ½" shingle overhang for standard 12" shingles. *Tip: Use blue chalk rather than red. Red chalk will stain roofing materials.*

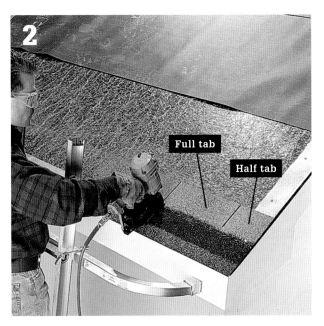

Full tab

Half tab

Trim off one-half (6") of an end tab on a shingle. Position the shingle upside down, so the tabs are aligned with the chalk line and the half-tab is flush against the rake edge. Drive ⅞" roofing nails near each end, 1" down from each slot between tabs. Butt a full upside-down shingle next to the trimmed shingle, and nail it. Fill out the row, trimming the last shingle flush with the opposite rake edge.

Apply the first full course of shingles over the starter course with the tabs pointing down. Begin at the rake edge where you began the starter row. Place the first shingle so it overhangs the rake edge by ⅜" and the eaves edge by ½". Make sure the top of each shingle is flush with the top of the starter course, following the chalk line.

Snap a chalk line from the eaves edge to the ridge to create a vertical line to align the shingles. Choose an area with no obstructions, as close as possible to the center of the roof. The chalk line should pass through a slot or a shingle edge on the first full shingle course. Use a carpenter's square to establish a line perpendicular to the eaves edge.

(continued)

5

18"

12"

6"

5" reveal

Use the vertical reference line to establish a shingle pattern with slots that are offset by 6" in succeeding courses. Tack down a shingle 6" to one side of the vertical line, 5" above the bottom edge of the first-course shingles to start the second row. Tack down shingles for the third and fourth courses, 12" and 18" from the vertical line. Butt the fifth course against the line.

6

Fill in shingles in the second through fifth courses, working upward from the second course and maintaining a consistent 5" reveal. Slide lower-course shingles under any upper-course shingles left partially nailed, and then nail them down. *Tip: Install roof jacks, if needed, after filling out the fifth course.*

7

Check the alignment of the shingles after each four-course cycle. In several spots on the last installed course, measure from the bottom edge of a shingle to the nearest felt paper line. If you discover any misalignment, make minor adjustments over the next few rows until it's corrected.

8

When you reach obstructions, such as dormers, install a full course of shingles above them so you can retain your shingle offset pattern. On the unshingled side of the obstruction, snap another vertical reference line using the shingles above the obstruction as a guide.

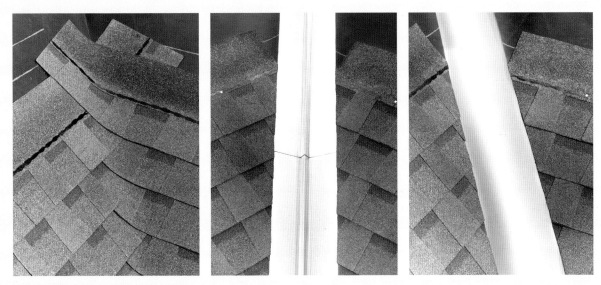

Here are three options for flashing a valley where two roof planes meet. Closed Valley (left): Create a seamless roof by first laying waterproof membrane in the valley, then mitering shingles at the top and overlapping in the valley. Open Valley (middle): Nail metal flashing down the intersection joint, and overlap shingles from both sides, at least 2". Terminate the flashing at the gutter and lay a bead of roofing cement along the joint between shingles and flashing. W-Flashed Valley (right): Special "W" channel flashing is used where two roofs with different pitches meet. The channel is attached to the roof decks with clips and the clips are bent up at bottom to deflect water back into the flashing.

Shingle upward from the eaves on the unshingled side of the obstruction using the vertical line as a reference for re-establishing your shingle slot offset pattern. Fill out the shingle courses past the rake edges of the roof, then trim off the excess.

Trim off excess shingle material at the V in the valley flashing using a utility knife and straightedge. Do not cut into the flashing. The edges will be trimmed back farther at a slight taper after both roof decks are completely shingled.

(continued)

Install shingles on adjoining roof decks, starting at the bottom edge using the same offset alignment pattern shown in steps 1 to 6. Install shingles until courses overlap the center of the valley flashing. Trim shingles at both sides of the valley when finished.

Install shingles up to the vent pipe so the flashing rests on at least one row of shingles. Apply a heavy double bead of roofing cement along the bottom edge of the flange.

Sleeve

Place the flashing over the vent pipe. Position the flashing collar so the longer portion of the tapered neck slopes down the roof and the flange lies over the shingles. Nail the perimeter of the flange using rubber gasket nails.

Cut shingles to fit around the neck of the flashing so they lie flat against the flange. Do not drive roofing nails through the flashing. Instead, apply roofing cement to the back of shingles where they lie over the flashing.

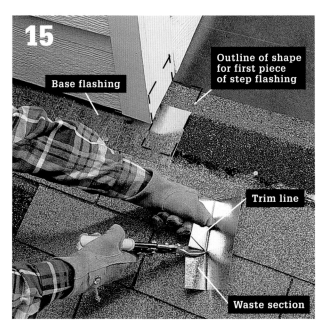

Shingle up to an element that requires flashing so the top of the reveal areas are within 5" of the element. Install base flashing using the old base flashing as a template. Bend a piece of step flashing in half and set it next to the lowest corner of the element. Mark a trim line on the flashing, following the vertical edge of the element. Cut the flashing to fit.

Pry out the lowest courses of siding and any trim at the base of the element. Insert spacers to prop the trim or siding away from the work area. Apply roofing cement to the base flashing in the area where the overlap with the step flashing will be formed. Tuck the trimmed piece of step flashing under the propped area, and secure the flashing. Fasten the flashing with one rubber gasket nail driven near the top and into the roof deck.

Apply roofing cement to the top side of the first piece of step flashing where it will be covered by the next shingle course. Install the shingle by pressing it firmly into the roofing cement. Do not nail through the flashing underneath.

Tuck another piece of flashing under the trim or siding, overlapping the first piece of flashing at least 2". Set the flashing into roofing cement applied on the top of the shingle. Nail the shingle in place without driving nails through the flashing. Install flashing up to the top of the element the same way. Trim the last piece of flashing to fit the top corner of the element. Reattach the siding and trim.

(continued)

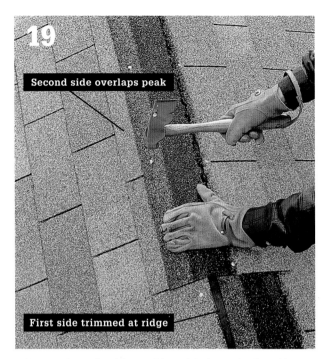

19

Second side overlaps peak

First side trimmed at ridge

20

When you reach a hip or ridge, shingle up the first side until the top of the uppermost reveal area is within 5" of the hip or ridge. Trim the shingles along the peak. Install shingles on the opposite side of the hip or ridge. Overlap the peak no more than 5".

Cut three 12"-sq. cap shingles from each three-tab shingle. With the back surface facing up, cut the shingles at the tab lines. Trim the top corners of each square with an angled cut, starting just below the seal strip to avoid overlaps in the reveal area.

21

22

Snap a chalk line 6" down from the ridge, parallel to the peak. Attach cap shingles, starting at one end of the ridge, aligned with the chalk line. Drive two 1¼" roofing nails per cap about 1" from each edge, just below the seal strip.

Following the chalk line, install cap shingles halfway along the ridge, creating a 5" reveal for each cap. Then, starting at the opposite end, install caps over the other half of the ridge to meet the first run in the center. Cut a 5"-wide section from the reveal area of a shingle tab, and use it as a "closure cap" to cover the joint where the caps meet.

23

Shingle the hips in the same manner using a chalk reference line and cap shingles. Start at the bottom of each hip and work to the peak. Where hips join with roof ridges, install a custom shingle cut from the center of a cap shingle. Set the cap at the end of the ridge and bend the corners so they fit over the hips. Secure each corner with a roofing nail, and cover the nail heads with roofing cement.

Option: Install a ridge vent all along the roof ridge to create ventilation. A ridge vent is usually made of a strip of loosely woven batting that allows airflow. This is installed over long slots that are cut into the roof on both sides next to the ridge. Some ridge vents have a granular mineral surface that matches your shingle color preattached; other are designed to be shingled over as you would a normal roof ridge.

24

After all shingles are installed, trim them at the valleys to create a gap that's 3" wide at the top and widens at a rate of ⅛" per foot as it moves downward. Use a utility knife and straightedge to cut the shingles, making sure not to cut through the valley flashing. At the valleys, seal the undersides and edges of shingles with roofing cement. Also cover exposed nail heads with roofing cement.

25

Mark and trim the shingles at the rake edges of the roof. Snap a chalk line ⅜" from the edge to make an overhang, then trim the shingles.

Sheathing Exterior Walls

Wall sheathing is the skin that serves as a base for the final siding. There are basically two types of sheathing—structural and non-structural. Structural sheathing supports the framing, increasing the overall strength of the structure. Non-structural sheathing is used where the structure is supported in other ways such as metal ties or let-in boards. The category includes insulation panels and other lightweight alternatives.

Structural sheathing is the option of choice in most additions, and in most cases that means using plywood or oriented-strand board (OSB). Regardless of which you choose, the sheets should be rated for exterior wall use. The most common size is ½ inch, although local code requirements may call for different thicknesses.

Although the standard dimensions for sheets are 4 × 8 feet, you can also purchase 4 × 9 feet, 4 × 10 feet, or even 4 × 12 feet sheets to accommodate your needs. Many people choose to install the panels before raising the walls into position, which makes it easier to work with the large panels, but heavier lifting. Installing the panels after the walls are up, however, makes marking the cuts for window and door openings easier and faster.

Tools & Materials ▸

Hammer	8d nails
Circular saw	4 × 8 OSTS sheets
Reciprocating saw	2 × 4 blocking

Plywood or OSB panels that are rated for use as wall sheathing are a much better choice for exterior addition walls than insulation boards or other panels that may be allowed but have little or no structural value.

Plywood versus OSB Wall Sheathing ▸

The most common wall sheathing materials are plywood, which is formed of laminated wood layers, and OSB, made of wood strands mixed with adhesive. These two types of sheathing are interchangeable, but in most areas of the country, OSB is cheaper. OSB can also be formed into much larger panels than plywood can, making it a good choice for unusually large wall surfaces. However, plywood absorbs water and dries in a much more efficient and uniform fashion. This means it's a better option in high-moisture areas and as a base for some types of siding such as stucco and wood shingles.

How to Install Wall Sheathing

Nail the first full panel into place, starting at a bottom corner. If it works for your layout and situation, install the panels horizontally to cut down on trips up and down the ladder. Space nails at 6" intervals around the edges and every 12" in the field.

Start installing the second row of sheathing panels with a half sheet to stagger the joints between panels. Leave a ⅛" expansion gap horizontally and ¹⁄₁₆" gap vertically.

Measure carefully and then mark and cut the openings for windows, doors, and other openings such as vents. In many cases, you may find it easier to trace around framed openings after the sheathing is installed and then cut them out with a reciprocating saw.

Option: Install 4 × 9 ft. sheets of sheathing in installations where the sheathing needs to fill past the wall top plate and up to or near the rafter tops.

Building Wrap

Housewrap is a specially engineered fabric that blocks air and water infiltration from the outside but allows moisture vapor to pass through from the inside. It's best to apply the housewrap before installing windows and doors, but since that's not always possible with a remodeling or siding replacement job, you can cut the housewrap to fit around them. Most siding materials need to be nailed to studs, and the marks on the housewrap identify their locations. Staples are permissible for fastening housewrap, but cap nails are recommended and have better holding power.

Felt paper is not the same as housewrap. It's not necessarily designed to work as an air barrier, and it may absorb water. Do not substitute felt paper when housewrap is supposed to be used.

Tools & Materials ▸

Hammer
Utility knife
Tape dispenser
Cap nails (2" or 3")

Housewrap (3', 5', 9', or 10' widths)
Housewrap tape

Make "martini glass" cutouts in the building wrap for window and vent openings. Fold the flaps inside and staple along studs and sill.

How to Install Building Wrap

Starting 6 to 12" around a corner and 3" over the foundation to cover the sill plate, unroll the housewrap along the side of the house with the printed side facing out. Align the printed stud marks on the housewrap with the stud marks on the sheathing. Keep the roll straight as you unwrap it.

Nail the housewrap every 12 to 18" on the vertical stud lines using cap nails. Keep the housewrap pulled snug as it's unrolled. Cut holes in the housewrap for extrusions such as hose spigots and the electric meter.

When starting a new roll, overlap vertical seams by 6 to 12", aligning the stud marks. Begin the second course by overlapping the bottom course by 6". Once again, make sure stud marks are lined up.

At window and door locations, cut the housewrap at the middle of the nailing flanges. At the bottom, cut the housewrap at the sill. Pull the sill and jamb flashing over the housewrap. Be careful not to slice the nailing flanges and windowsills when cutting the housewrap.

Tape all seams with insulation tape to assist the vapor seal.

Also apply insulation tape to accidental tears, and seams around doors, windows, and plumbing and electrical protrusions using housewrap tape. Tape the bottom of the protrusion first, then the sides, then place a piece of tape over the top.

Installing Siding

The best way to seamlessly blend the addition with the rest of the house is to use the exact same siding for the addition. However, the transition will be convincing only if the siding runs from the house to the addition without visual interruption. The following illustrations demonstrate how to integrate your new siding with your old as naturally as possible.

Vinyl, fiber cement, or wood clapboard: Although the mounting method is different for siding and clapboard, the method for incorporating old with new is the same: on parallel walls, remove short end sections and panels, pry up starter strips, and overlap building wrap from the addition onto the old wall. Replace the siding with new full-length pieces that run onto the addition wall. On inside corners, run inside corner trim up the intersection and side the addition as new.

Stucco: Stucco is a difficult material to work with at any time, but blending two stucco walls is a challenge usually best left to a professional. The trick is to score and hammer out several inches at the end of the existing wall. Leave the steel mesh lath, and overlap with the lath from the new wall. Then stucco the joint carefully to avoid cracks.

Brick and stone: There are two methods for incorporating the brick or stone wall of a new wall with an older surface. The most solid connection is made by "toothing" out the existing wall—removing bricks or stones along the edge and cementing in connecting pieces from new wall to old. On irregular stone walls or where you want to save the labor of toothing a brick wall, you can use steel wall ties. These are rails that are attached to the existing wall with tongues that are hooked in and sit between the mortar joints of the new wall.

Shingles and shakes: Pry up shingles 1 foot in from the edge (leaving only whole shingles) at which the parallel addition wall will attach. Overlap addition wall building wrap and begin installing shingles from the exposed part of the existing wall, repeating the existing pattern. Where the walls meet at a right angle use inside corner trim and shingle the addition wall as you would any new construction.

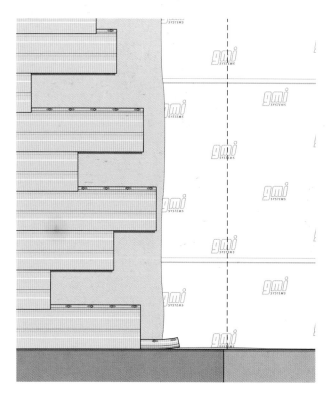

Lap siding to lap siding

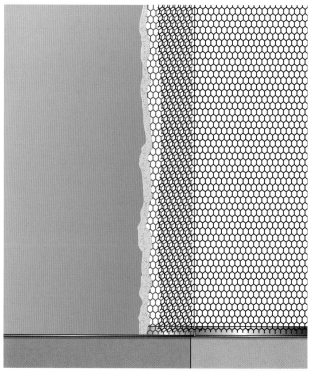

Stucco to stucco

Masonry unit to masonry unit

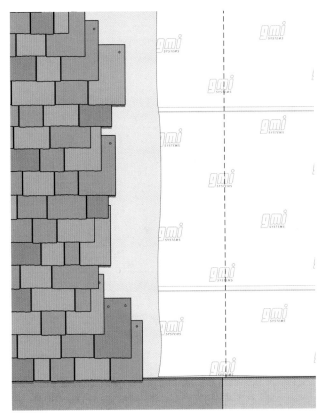

Shingle to shingle

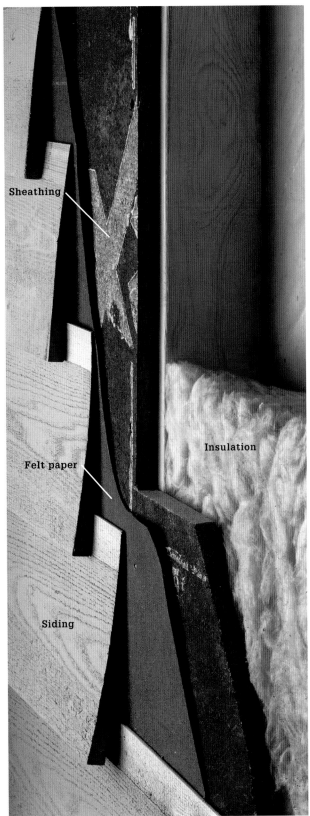

Lap siding, backers for stucco, furring strips for shakes, and any panelized siding products should be attached with fasteners that go through the sheathing and into the wall framing.

How to Install Vinyl Siding

Nail the inside and outside corner posts for the siding into place, starting ¼" below top of corners. Drive nails in on either side of each post and check for plumb, then nail every 8" down the post, overlapping the top pieces. Leave a gap between the nails and the surface of the siding so that the post is loose enough to move slightly.

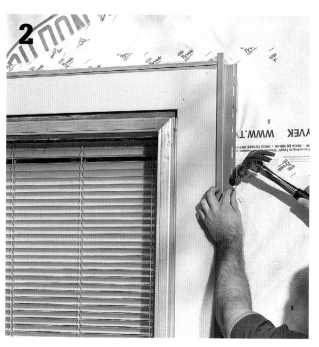

Measure, cut, and nail J-channels in place on either side of windows and doors, in the same manner that you nailed the corner posts, leaving them slightly loose to allow for expansion.

Cut a 1"-long piece of J-channel for the top corner of each window and door. Bend over the flange of each cut corner piece slightly so it fits over the top J-channel and functions as a drip edge.

Measure, cut, and install J-channel along the roof lines. To overlap, cut 1" from the nailing hem. Overlap ¾", leaving ¼" for expansion.

5

At an outside corner, measure up from the point where the bottom edge of the siding will hang to the width of the starter strip minus ¼". Hammer in a nail at this point and repeat at the opposite corner. Snap a chalk line between nails as a reference for starter strips.

6

Measure and snap starter strip chalk lines around the other walls of the addition. Position the starter strip so that top edges are even with the reference chalk lines. Fasten the starter strips by hammering nails in the centers of the slots at 10" intervals.

7

Securely lock the first horizontal siding panel into the starter strip. Ensure that the panel is locked in over its entire length before nailing. Nail the first panel to the sheathing. Hammer nails in the centers of slots, leaving a 1⁄32" gap between the nailheads and the siding surfaces.

8

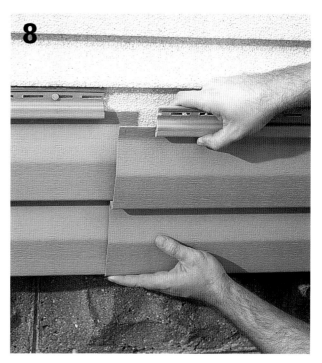

Check that the panel can move freely from side to side. Continue nailing panels as needed to complete the course. Overlap adjacent panels by approximately 1", or about one-half the length of the notch at the end of the panel.

(continued)

9

Lock and nail the panels for the second course into place. Stagger the panel lengths so that the overlaps are offset by at least 12" from course to course. Check alignment and level after every course and make adjustments as necessary.

10

Measure and cut panels to fit around the openings, leaving an extra ¼" all around for expansion. At cutout areas beneath an opening, punch the upper cut edge of the panel with a snap lock punch and nail through the hole. Install utility trim over the edge.

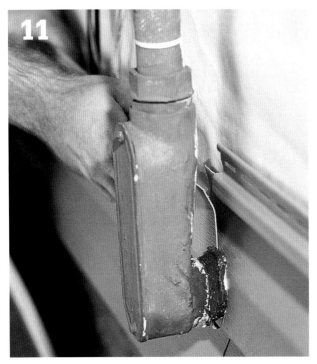

11

Cut slots in the panels to fit around fixtures such as a hose bibb or a service entry cable housing, leaving an extra ¼" around the fixture. Add a decorative trim ring, available at home centers or your siding retailer, for a finished look.

Blending Old & New ▸

Making the siding on your addition blend with the existing siding, and look good in its own right, is mostly a matter of using a few simple design techniques. Overlap panels as far away as possible from doorways and other areas that see significant foot traffic. This will place vertical seams where they are less noticeable. And to keep unsightly seams to a minimum, use panels that are as long as possible and never shorter than 3 ft.

Other Types of Lap Siding

Wood lap siding comes in wide or narrow strips and is normally beveled. Exterior-rated wood that can be clear coated is common (usually cedar or redwood). Other wood types are used, too, but these are usually sold preprimed and are suitable for painting only.

Fiber-cement lap siding is a relative newcomer but its use is spreading quickly. It is very durable but requires some special tools for cutting and installation.

Starting Wood & Fiber Cement Lap Siding ▸

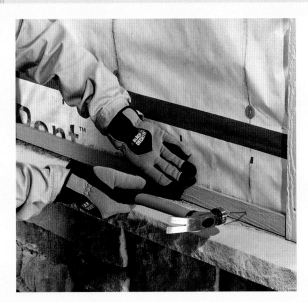

Attach a starter strip at the base of each wall section. Cut the strip from the top (narrow) edge of the worst-looking pieces of siding. Nail the strip all along the bottom of the wall, keeping a gap of about ⅛" beneath it to limit contact with moisture.

Nail the first course of beveled siding in place. For fiber cement board drive nails only through the area of the siding board that will be overlapped by the next course, which will conceal the nailhead.

Soffits, Fascia & Gutters

Some older homes and certain house styles such as Arts & Crafts are designed with open eaves in which the ends of the rafters are exposed. But installing fascia and soffits creates a finished appearance to the roofline.

In addition, modern vinyl soffits offer many advantages over traditional wood styles; they are easy to clean, simple to install, and virtually maintenance-free. Vinyl panels and channels are easily cut to fit with special shears or a saw. The soffit panels come in solid and perforated styles and, although the standard practice is to install one perforated panel for about every three or four solid panels, you can actually create an entire soffit of perforated panels—which will make ordering the materials much easier.

Soffit & Fascia Types

Fascia cladding. Clad an existing fascia with aluminum or vinyl, or nail F-channel to the bottom of the fascia if you prefer to maintain the wood surface. You can also select vinyl fascia, with the soffit channel molded into the design.

Metal soffit panels. Nail F-channel to the wall, leaving a small gap between the nailhead and channel to allow for expansion. Soffit panels rest on a fascia cladding ledge and F-channel. A portion of each panel is usually perforated for ventilation.

Wood soffits. Wood panels are custom cut from ¼" or ½" exterior rated plywood. The panels can be nailed to rafter lookouts or set onto narrow ledges similar to F-channels. Vent covers are attached over ventilation holes cut into the panels.

How to Install Gutters & Downspouts

Mark the starting point of the gutter at one end (or the middle of a long run), and at the low point at the other end, allowing for ¼" to ½" to slope for every 10 ft. of run. Snap a chalk line between the two points.

Attach a drop outlet to the fascia at the low point, preferably with a long deck screw that extends into the rafter end.

Mount hangers for the gutters, beginning at the high-end mark. Mount the hangers approximately every 30" unless directed otherwise by the manufacturer.

Cut the gutter sections and downspouts to fit using a fine-toothed hacksaw. Remove any burrs with fine-grade sandpaper and test-fit the sections.

Build the downspout by connecting the pipe sections with elbows to run down the wall. Connect the downspout to the wall with straps spaced approximately at 8 ft. intervals.

Complete the downspout assembly with a final elbow and pipe section, routed onto a splash drain or into a drain culvert so that water drains away from the foundation.

Installing Windows

Preventing water from getting in is one of the most important considerations when installing a window in an addition. The key is to seal all joints around the window and block anyplace the water could wick in. Although caulking can be effective, it's also easy to miss small spots, and caulking will deteriorate over time. That's why builders in wetter parts of the country install plenty of flashing around the window with waterproof membrane. If you want extra protection against water infiltration, start from the bottom, cut strips of self-adhesive waterproof membrane, and apply them under the window, up the sides, and then on top of the window. All seams should face down and the top and bottom strips should run out 6 inches on either side of the window. Repeat the procedure over the nailing flanges.

Tools & Materials ▸

Hammer	Brickmold
Tape measure	Roofing nails
Level	Expanding
Utility knife	foam insulation
Handsaw	
Caulk gun	
Window	
Self-adhesive flashing	
Exterior-grade	
silicone caulk	
Shims	
Flashing	

Mullion post

New windows can be installed after the wall framing and sheathing is done. Many builders sheath over the window openings, then cut them out as they install each window, to keep weather and wildlife out.

Green Window Choices ▸

Installing the right windows for your home and region can instantly trim your energy usage. That's why, when choosing windows for an addition, you should always look for the Energy Star label. A designation given by the U.S. Department of Energy, the Energy Star label ensures a window meets or exceeds federal guidelines for home energy efficiency. An even more important gauge than simply looking for an Energy Star label is to read the NFRC label on the window. Specifically, note the U-factor and Solar Heat Gain Coefficient (SHGC) ratings for the window. If you live in a fairly cold region of the country, you want the lowest U-factor you can find, with a moderate to high SHGC. If your home is located in a temperate area with consistently warm temperatures, the SHGC number is the most important one to you, and it should be as low as possible.

How to Install a Window

Flash the rough sill. Apply 9"-wide self-adhesive flashing tape to the rough sill to prevent moisture infiltration below the window. Install the flashing tape so it wraps completely over the sill and extends 10 to 12" up the jack studs. Fold the rest of the tape over the housewrap to create a 3" overlap. Peel off the backing and press the tape firmly in place. Install tape on the side jambs butting up to the header, and then flash the header.

Caulk the opening. Apply a ½"-wide bead of caulk around the outside edges of the jack studs and header to seal the window flange in the opening. Leave the rough sill uncaulked to allow any water that may penetrate the flashing to drain out.

(continued)

Position the window. Set the window unit into the rough opening, and center it side to side. Check the sill for level.

Tack the top corners. Drive a roofing nail through each top corner hole of the top window flange to tack it in place. Do not drive the rest of the nails into the top flange yet.

Plumb the window. Have a helper hold the window in place from outside while you work inside. Check the window jamb for square by measuring from corner to corner. If the measurements are the same, the jamb is square. Insert shims between the side jambs and rough opening near the top corners to hold the jambs in position. Use additional shims as needed to bring the jamb into square. Recheck the diagonals after shimming.

Nail the flanges. Drive 2" roofing nails through the flange nailing holes and into the rough sill to secure it. Handnail this flange, being careful not to damage the flange or window cladding.

Flash the side flanges. Seal the side flanges with flashing tape, starting 4 to 6" below the sill flashing and ending 4 to 6" above the top flange. Press the tape firmly in place.

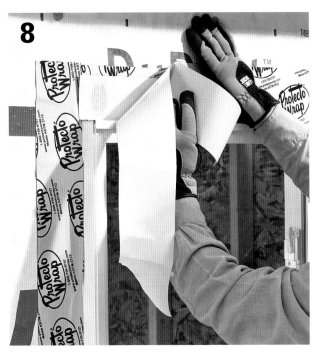

Install the drip cap. Cut a piece of metal drip edge to fit over the top window jamb. This is particularly important if your new window has an unclad wooden jamb with preinstalled brickmold. Set the drip edge in place on the top jamb, and secure the flange with a strip of wide flashing tape. Do not nail it. Overlap the side flashing tape by 6". *Note: If you plan to trim the window with wood brickmold or other moldings, install the drip edge above that trim instead.*

Finish the installation. Cut the shim ends so they are flush with the inside of the wall using a utility knife or handsaw.

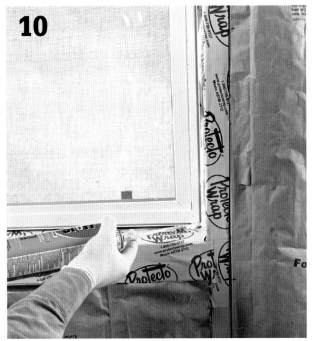

Spray non-expanding foam insulation for windows and doors around the perimeter of the window on the interior side.

Installing an Entry Door

If your addition is to the front of your house and includes an entry, the new entry door will provide you with a fine opportunity to dress up the house and to integrate the new part with the old. Your choice of exterior door design should be driven by the style of the exterior doors on the existing house. Matching door styles is just one more way of integrating the addition with the design of the house. In addition to the number of panels or other design elements, you'll need to determine whether you want an "inswing" or "outswing" door, and what "hand" it should be. This is a matter of space and precedent. Most exterior doors swing in, but if your addition's space will be small and cluttered, you may want to opt for an outswing door. The "hand" of the door is simply the location of the handle on the side the door swings toward. For example, a left handed inswing door will have the handle on the left side as you face it from inside the space. The hand of the door should be determined by practicality; if there is a perpendicular wall right next to the door, the door should open on the side away from the wall so that visitors don't feel crowded upon entering.

If your addition is in the rear of the house, it may contain an entry door that is less of a design statement than simply a serviceable way to get in and out. The following service door installation includes a fairly plain steel door leading to a workshop addition. If you are installing a fancier front door, the techniques are fundamentally the same.

Tools & Materials ▸

Handsaw	Exterior-grade
Hammer	silicone caulk
Caulk gun	Galvanized
Prehung exterior door	casing nails
Brick mold	Self-adhesive
Shims	flashing tape

How to Install a Prehung Entry Door

Flash the bottom and sides. Apply two strips of self-adhesive flashing tape to cover the jack studs in the door's rough opening. Cut a slit in the tape and extend the outer ear 4 to 6" past the bottom edge of the header. Fold the tape over the housewrap to create a 3" overlap. Peel off the backing and press the tape firmly in place.

Flash the header. Cover the header with a third piece of self-adhesive flashing tape, extending the ends of the tape 6" beyond the side flashing. Fold the extra tape over the housewrap to form a 3" overlap.

Seal the opening. Apply a ½"-wide bead of caulk up the outside edges of the jack stud area and around the header to seal the brickmold casing.

Position the door in the opening. Set the bottoms of the side jambs inside the rough opening, and tip the door into place. Adjust the door so it's level, plumb, and centered in the opening.

Attach the door. Drive 2½" galvanized casing nails through the brickmold to fasten the door to the jack studs and header. Space the nails every 12".

Shim at the dead bolt and behind the hinges. Insert pairs of shims with the door closed, adjusting the shims in or out until there's a consistent ⅛" gap between the door and the jamb. If your door came with them, insert one long screw at each hinge into the framing. Then fill the gap with non-expanding foam.

Wiring an Addition

Your complete building plans must include a detailed wiring plan that clearly outlines placement and technical data for all outlets and fixtures in the space. In most cases, a new addition will be wired with multiple new circuits and perhaps even its own subpanel. The cable for the new circuits should be run after the wall framing members are erected but before the wall surface coverings are installed.

Because installing wiring and making electrical hookups is an inherently dangerous activity, hiring a professional electrical contractor is always the best option. Along with the assurance that the work will be completed safely, another advantage to using a pro is that they will take care of all of the permit application and inspections coordination—no small task in some cases.

If you are an experienced DIYer there is nothing stopping you from doing your own electrical work, but you must involve your local building department at every phase of the project. You will need to submit detailed plans to the electrical inspections department and pay a fee to obtain a permit for doing the work. Following all applicable wiring codes, you may then run cable and make hookups at receptacles, switches, and fixtures as needed. But you must have your work inspected before you can make live connections to the service panel, whether you are hooking up new circuits or adding a subpanel that is wired with multiple circuits to the new addition. You may not install wallcoverings until this inspection is done and your work is passed. Most areas require a final inspection after wallcoverings are installed and all hookups have been made.

The information in this chapter concerns the mechanical aspects of running electrical cable through walls to get from your service panel to the receptacles, switches, and electrical fixtures in your new addition. You will also find some basic instructions on making wiring connections to switches and receptacles. For more advanced tasks, such as adding new circuits to your service panel or wiring an electrical subpanel, additional information is required and professional guidance is recommended.

Tools & Materials ▸

Right-angle drill and spade or auger bits	Multimeter or circuit tester
Cable ripping tool	Cable staples
Wire stripping tool	NM cable
Hammer	Cable clamps
Lineman's pliers	Electrical boxes
Needlenose pliers	Wire connectors
Screwdriver	Cable protector plates
	Touchless circuit tester

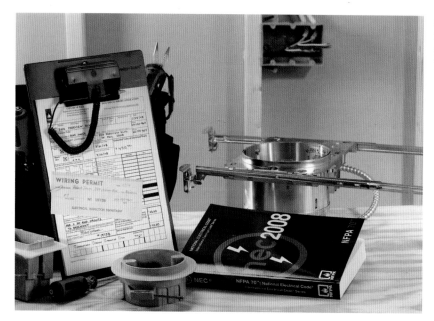

Any wiring project is a serious job that requires considerable experience and oversight, including a permit and on-site inspections from your municipality.

Know Your Cable ▸

With very rare exceptions, the cable you'll use in wiring your addition is known as "NM" or non-metallic cable. This has been the standard for home wiring systems since 1965. The outer sheath of the cable, made from rugged polyvinyl chloride, is labeled with the number and gauge of the wires inside, not counting the grounding wire. For instance, a cable labeled "14/2" holds two insulated 14-gauge wires, plus the bare copper grounding wire. The outer sheath is also stamped with the maximum voltage rating as determined by Underwriters Laboratories. Special strippers are used to strip both the outside sheath and individual wires; be sure to leave extra when cutting cable to length; you can always cut it back and splicing cables may only be done in an approved junction box that is accessible after the wallcoverings are installed. Refer to your wiring plan to make sure each length of cable is correct for the circuit size and configuration.

Building codes allow you to use 14-gauge cable for 15-amp circuits, but not for 20-amp circuits. Many professionals use 12-gauge wire. It costs a bit more, is a little harder to manipulate and it may require you to upgrade to larger electrical boxes to comply with fill capacity codes. All codes require 12-gauge copper wire for 20-amp circuits.

Sheathed nonmetallic (NM) cable is used to run new circuits that supply electricity to your addition. The heavier-duty 12-gauge cable can be recognized instantly by its yellow PVC jacket.

Electrical Box and Cable Positioning ▸

The placement of electrical cable and boxes is tightly regulated by code, which was developed to minimize the risk of fire or life-threatening shock. Electrical boxes should be mounted at consistent heights: in living areas, this means boxes should be located 12" on center from the top of the finished floor, and switches should be 48" from the finished floor. The measurements can be altered to accommodate special circumstances such as a child's bedroom or living quarters for a disabled person. Cables should be anchored with staples within 8" of each box and each 4 ft. thereafter when running along studs. Always form smooth curves and take care not to crimp electrical cable or run it diagonally between framing members. Cables running through studs should be about 20" above the floor.

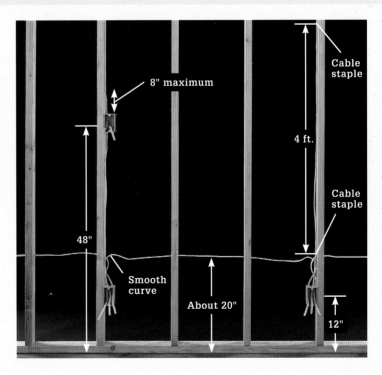

How to Install Electrical Boxes

Mark the location of each receptacle box, usually about 12" above floor level, on center, for outlets.

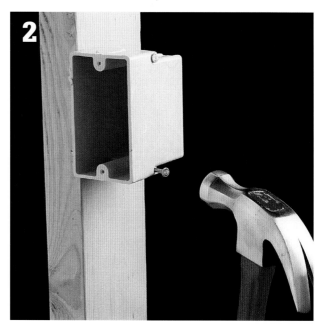

Nail electrical boxes in position. The front should be flush with the finished wall. For instance, if you are installing ½" drywall, the box should project out from the stud face by ½". Look for depth marks on the box.

Use a hammer and screwdriver to open one knockout for each cable that will enter the box. *Note: Some nonmetallic electrical boxes are made with barbed clamps instead of knockouts. These clamps should be left intact.*

48"

Position electrical boxes for light switches on the latch side of doors and at other accessible locations. A typical height for switches is 48" from the floor to the center of the electrical box. In kitchens, however, 45" is more typical because it positions receptacles in the middle of the backsplash area between countertops and wall cabinets, and it is recommended that switches and above-counter receptacles be at the same height.

Wall Thickness ▸

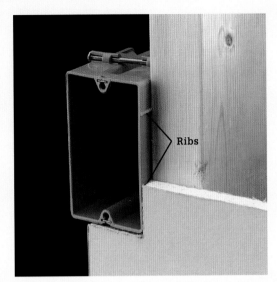

Integral ribs cast into many nonmetallic boxes are used to register the box against the wall studs so the front edges of the box will be flush with the wall surface after drywall is installed. Most are set for ½" drywall, but if your wall will be a different thickness you may be able to find a box with corresponding ribs. Otherwise, use a piece of the wallcovering material as a reference.

Box Position ▸

Electrical boxes in adjacent rooms should be positioned close together when they share a common wall and are controlled by the same circuit. This simplifies the cable installations and also reduces the amount of cable needed.

5

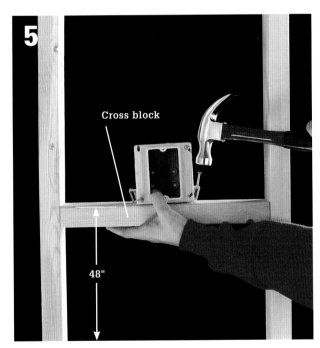

Install a switch box between studs by toenailing a piece of 2 × 4 blocking between the wall studs. Nail the box to the top of the block, so that the face of the box will be flush with final wall surface.

6

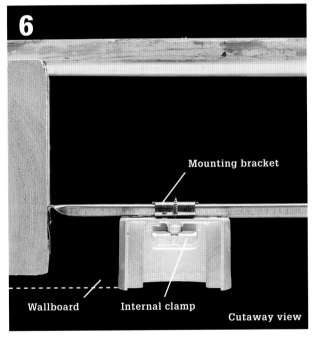

Mount lighting fixture boxes between joists by attaching the box to an adjustable brace bar. Nail the ends to the joists so the face of the box will be flush with the finished ceiling surface. Use internal cable clamps when using a box with a brace bar.

Running Electrical Cable

Drill ⅝" holes through studs for cable. A corded right-angle drill with a ⅝"-dia. spade bit is the best tool for this job but cordless drills will work. Holes should be at least 1¼" in from the front edge of the stud, or metal plates should be nailed to the front edge of the stud.

Pull the cables through the holes once you've drilled all the holes at the same height. Prevent kinks by straightening the cable before pulling it through the holes.

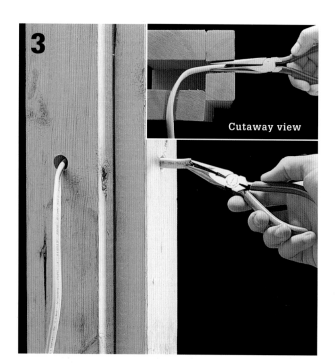

Form an L-shaped bend in the end of the cable so it can fit though a 90-degree turn, if need be, in corner framing. Insert the cable into one hole and pull it through the other hole with needlenose pliers (inset).

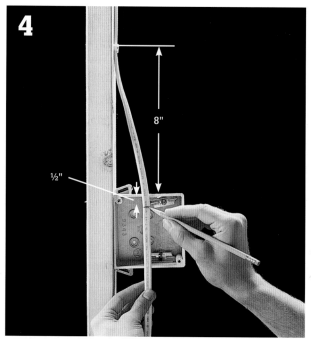

Staple the cable to the framing member 8" from the box. Mark the sheathing ½" past the box edge. Remove the sheathing from the mark to the end of the cable and cut off excess. Insert the cable through the knockout.

How to Strip NM Sheathing & Insulation

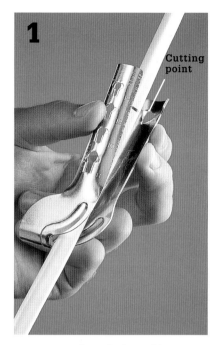

Measure and mark the cable 8 to 10" from the end. Slide the cable ripper onto the cable, and squeeze it firmly to force the cutting point through the plastic sheathing.

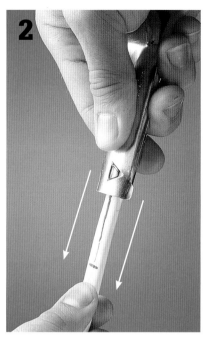

Grip the cable tightly with one hand, and pull the cable ripper toward the end of the cable to cut open the plastic sheathing.

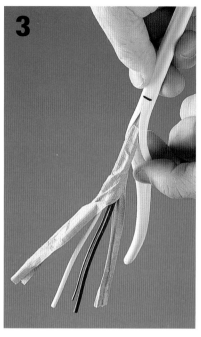

Peel back the plastic sheathing and the paper wrapping from the individual wires.

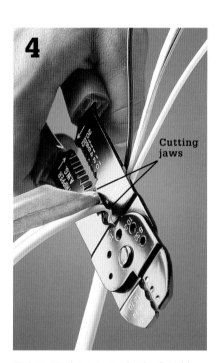

Cut away the excess plastic sheathing and paper wrapping, using the cutting jaws of a combination tool.

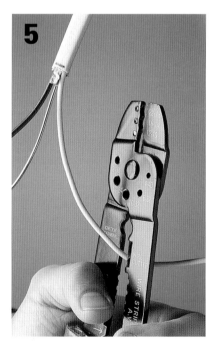

Cut individual wires as needed using the cutting jaws of the combination tool.

Strip insulation for each wire, using the stripper openings. Choose the opening that matches the gauge of the wire, and take care not to nick or scratch the ends of the wires.

How to Connect Wires to Screw Terminals

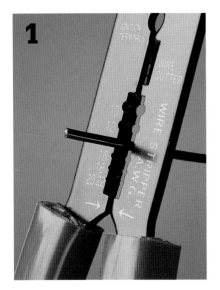

Strip about ¾" of insulation from each wire using a combination tool. Choose the stripper opening that matches the gauge of the wire, then clamp the wire in the tool. Pull the wire firmly to remove plastic insulation.

Form a C-shaped loop in the end of each wire using a needlenose pliers. The wire should have no scratches or nicks.

Hook each wire around the screw terminal so it forms a clockwise loop. Tighten screw firmly. Insulation should just touch the head of the screw. Never place the ends of two wires under a single screw terminal. Instead, use a pigtail wire (page 155).

How to Join Wires with a Connector

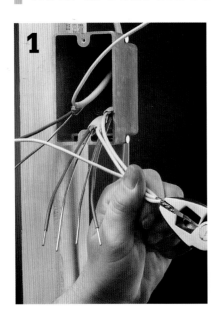

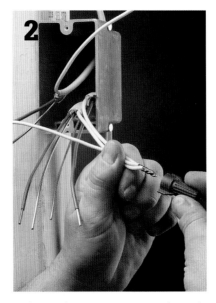

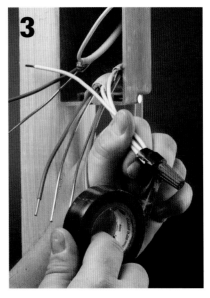

Ensure power is off. Grasp the wires to be joined in the jaws of a pair of linesman's pliers. The ends of the wires should be flush and they should be parallel and touching. Rotate the pliers clockwise two or three turns to twist the wire ends together.

Twist a wire connector over the ends of the wires. Make sure the connector is the right size. Hand-twist the connector as far onto the wires as you can. There should be no bare wire exposed beneath the collar of the connector. Do not overtighten the connector.

Option: Reinforce the connection by wrapping it with electrician's tape. By code, you cannot bind the wire joint with tape only, but it can be used as insurance. Few professional electricians use tape for purposes other than tagging wires for identification.

How to Pigtail Wires

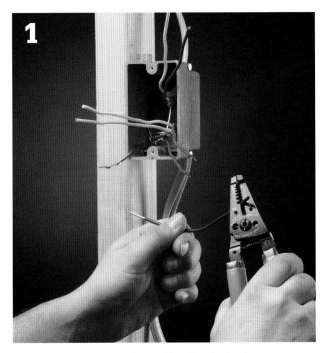

Cut a 6" length from a piece of insulated wire the same gauge and color as the wires it will be joining. Strip ¾" of insulation from each end of the insulated wire. *Note: Pigtailing is done mainly to avoid connecting multiple wires to one terminal, which is a code violation.*

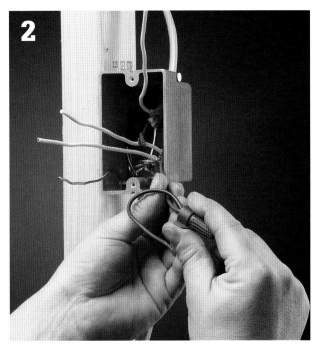

Join one end of the pigtail to the wires that will share the connection using a wire nut.

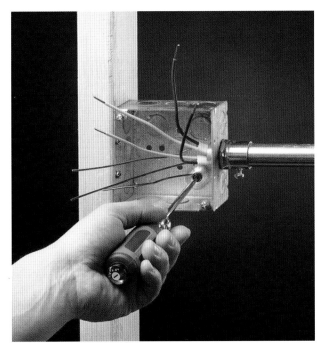

Alternative: If you are pigtailing to a grounding screw or grounding clip in a metal box, you may find it easier to attach one end of the wire to the grounding screw before you attach the other end to the other wires.

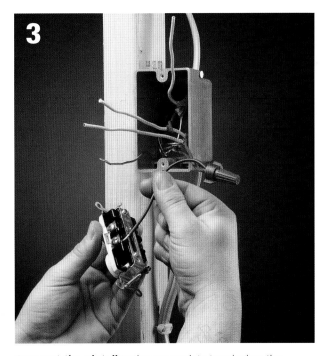

Connect the pigtail to the appropriate terminal on the receptacle or switch. Fold the wires neatly and press the fitting into the box.

Circuits for a Room Addition

The photo below shows the circuits you would likely want to install in a large room addition. This example shows the framing and wiring of an unfinished attic converted to an office or entertainment room with a bathroom. This room includes a subpanel and five new circuits plus telephone and cable-TV lines.

A wiring project of this sort is a potentially complicated undertaking that can be made simpler by breaking the project into convenient steps, and finishing one step before moving on to the next. Turn to pages 146 to 147 to see this project represented as a wiring diagram.

Individual Circuits

#1: Bathroom circuit. This 20-amp dedicated circuit supplies power to bathroom lights and fans, as well as receptacles that must be GFCI-protected at the box or at the receptacle. As with small appliance circuits in the kitchen, you may not tap into this circuit to feed any additional loads.

#2: Computer circuit. A 15-amp dedicated circuit with isolated ground is recommended, but an individual branch circuit is all that is required by most codes.

Circuit breaker subpanel receives power through a 10-gauge, three-wire feeder cable connected to a 30-amp,

14/2 cable

Vent fan

Circuit breaker subpanel

Vanity light fixture

GFCI receptacle

12/2 cable

12/2 cable

Time & light fixture switch

14/3 cable

Blower heater

10/3 cable

240-volt circuit breaker at the main circuit breaker panel. Larger room additions may require a 60-amp or a 100-amp feeder circuit breaker.

#3: Air-conditioner circuit. A 20-amp, 240-volt dedicated circuit. In cooler climates, or in a smaller room, you may need an air conditioner and circuit rated for only 120 volts.

#4: Basic lighting/receptacle circuit. This 15-amp, 120-volt circuit supplies power to most of the fixtures in the bedroom and study areas.

#5: Heater circuit. This 20-amp, 240-volt circuit supplies power to the bathroom blower-heater and to the baseboard heaters. Depending on the size of your room and the wattage rating of the baseboard heaters, you may need a 30-amp, 240-volt heating circuit.

Telephone outlet is wired with 22-gauge four-wire phone cable. If your home phone system has two or more separate lines, you may need to run a cable with eight wires, commonly called four-pair cable.

Cable television jack is wired with coaxial cable running from an existing television junction in the utility area.

14/3 cable

14/3 cable

Phone cable

Coaxial cable

These cables continue through the foreground wall to complete the circuits. This wall has been removed for clarity.

12/2 cable

14/2 cable

Diagram View

The diagram below shows the layout of the five circuits and the locations of their receptacles, switches, fixtures, and devices as shown in the photo on the previous pages. The circuits and receptacles are based on the needs of a 400-sq.-ft. space. An inspector will want to see a diagram like this one before issuing a permit. After you've received approval for your addition, the wiring diagram will serve as your guide as you complete your project.

■ **Circuit #1:** A 20-amp, 120-volt circuit serving the bathroom and closet area. Includes: 12/2 NM cable, double-gang box, timer switch, single-pole switch, 4 × 4" box with single-gang adapter plate, two plastic light fixture boxes, vanity light fixture, closet light fixture, 15-amp single-pole circuit breaker.

■ **Circuit #2:** A 15-amp, 120-volt computer circuit. Includes: 14/2 NM cable, single-gang box, 15-amp receptacle, 15-amp single-pole circuit breaker.

☐ **Circuit #3:** A 20-amp, 240-volt air-conditioner circuit. Includes: 12/2 NM cable; single-gang box; 20-amp,

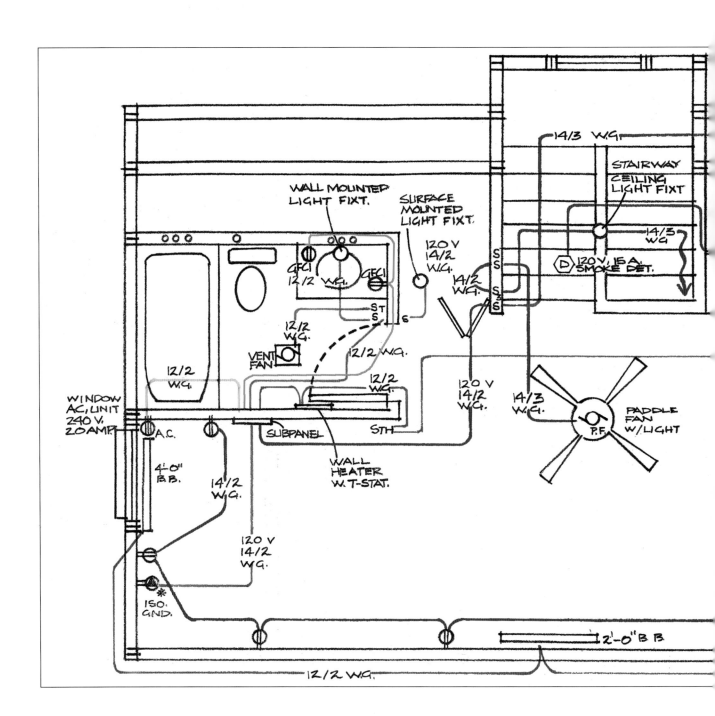

240-volt receptacle (duplex or singleplex style); 20-amp double-pole circuit.

Circuit #4: A 15-amp, 120-volt basic lighting/receptacle circuit serving most of the fixtures in the bedroom and study areas. Includes: 14/2 and 14/3 NM cable, two double-gang boxes, fan speed-control switch, dimmer switch, single-pole switch, two three-way switches, two plastic light fixture boxes, light fixture for stairway, smoke detector, metal light fixture box with brace bar, ceiling fan with light fixture, 10 single-gang boxes, 4 × 4" box with single-gang adapter plate, 10 duplex receptacles (15-amp), 15-amp single-pole circuit breaker.

Circuit #5: A 20-amp, 240-volt circuit that supplies power to three baseboard heaters controlled by a wall thermostat, and to a bathroom blower-heater controlled by a built-in thermostat. Includes: 12/2 NM cable, 750-watt blower heater, single-gang box, line-voltage thermostat, three baseboard heaters, 20-amp double-pole circuit breaker.

TV **Cable television jack:** Coaxial cable with F-connectors, signal splitter, cable television outlet with mounting brackets.

Circuit #6: A 20-amp, 120-volt, GFCI-protected small appliance circuit for the bathroom. Includes GFCI breaker, 14/2 NM cable, boxes, and 20-amp receptacles.

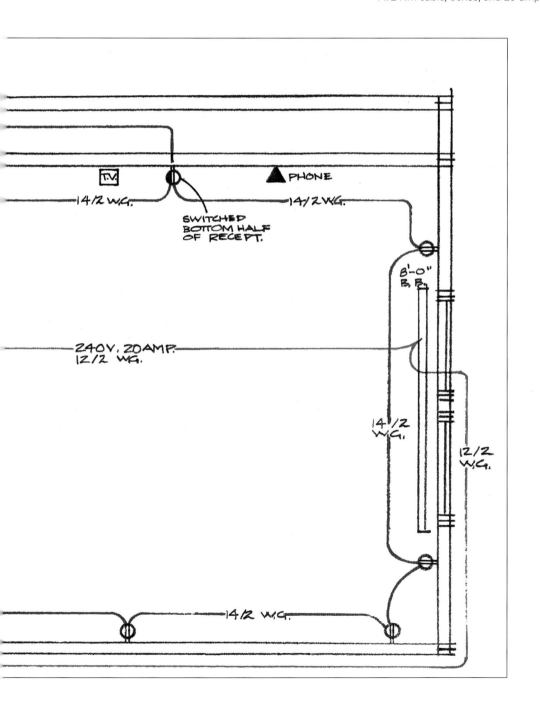

Plumbing the Addition

If your home addition includes a bathroom, sink, or fixture that consumes natural gas, you'll need to run pipes from the existing home service into the new space. Most homes are designed with plumbing features and pipes grouped together, which is why bathrooms are often on the floor above or next to a kitchen or existing bathroom. Ideally, an addition should be planned in the same way, so that new plumbing is as close as possible to existing pipes. This makes the actual installation of the new plumbing much easier.

The first lines you should run are the DWV (Drain, Waste, Venting) pipes and connections, because they are generally the largest and most cumbersome pipes in any plumbing system. As with all the plumbing, DWV pipes must be routed according to strict guidelines contained within plumbing codes. For instance, the allowable length of a pipeline serving a fixture trap is limited by the diameter of the pipe—if a longer run is necessary, you may need a pipe with a bigger diameter.

Although code requirements may seem excessively restrictive, they are actually practical rules developed to deal with the forces of gravity, air, and water pressure.

Pipe material is also standardized. DWV pipes are usually high-density plastic ABS (black) or PVC (white), while water supply pipes are copper. Additions onto older homes often require joining new pipe to older pipes of different materials. In most cases this isn't a problem—a PVC waste pipe can be connected to cast iron pipe or ABS using a banded coupling.

Regardless of what they're made of, pipes are run through the addition's walls in notches cut into framing members (or through holes in wider framing members). They can also be run below the floor in a crawlspace or basement. Attic conversions and second story additions involve running plumbing up through existing walls, and may even require opening up walls within the house to make connections. Check with the building inspector before cutting large holes in joists or load-bearing studs. Holes should generally be in the center third of the wood, and the diameter of the hole should be no more than ⅓ the width of the board.

Pipes that are routed under an addition's floor should run parallel to joists as much as possible, and should be secured in place with straps or hangers. Always use copper or plasic strap with the copper supply pipes.

A plumbed wall shows the correct way to run pipes—in cut-out notches in the studs, with metal protector plates nailed over the notches to protect the pipes. Copper supply pipes are run to the fixture position, and strapped to backing boards between the studs.

The Green Bathroom ▸

Toilet technology has come a long way since the traditional tank-fed gravity system first brought the bathroom indoors. Choose one of today's hi-tech toilets to conserve water.

Low-flow toilet technology has improved since the 1995 federal law went into effect requiring that all new toilets be limited to flushing with 1.6 gallons of water. Many new low-flow models use even less water per flush, and the result is a savings on the water bill and conservation of a precious natural resource.

Composting toilets go one step further, combining the toilet's output with wood chips to create fertilizer. Although expensive, these toilets use no water and put no load on sewer or septic systems thus reducing pollution.

Hot Water On Demand ▸

A sizable addition with a shower, sink, or dishwasher (or a combination of these) can quickly overwhelm the capacity of your home's hot water heater. But installing a new hot water heater or one dedicated to servicing the addition can mean a lot of extra plumbing, work, and expense. A great alternative for supplying hot water just to the addition is a tankless water heater. The unit is simply plumbed into the cold water supply line, providing heated water when it's needed. Because there is no tank, the tankless system saves the energy that would be required to heat water that is being stored for future use (and the attendant energy cost).

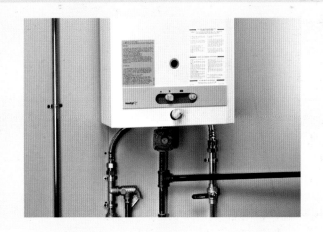

Heating and Cooling an Addition

The challenge in heating and cooling a home addition is to ensure that the space will be comfortable year round without adversely affecting the heating, cooling, and ventilation (HVAC) characteristics of the rest of the house. If the capacity of the furnace and central air conditioning is large enough, the new space can be heated and cooled by the existing system. If, however, the new space is too large to effectively tie into an existing HVAC system, you'll have to install a localized HVAC solution.

The heating and cooling needs of your new space will be affected by your climate. If you live in a cool area, air conditioning may not even be a concern, whereas a highly efficient heating system will be essential for keeping energy costs down and making the space comfortable. In southern states, the delivery of heat is secondary to air conditioning and ventilation. The type of addition has an impact as well. A room addition will have roughly the same heating and cooling characteristics as the rest of the house. An attic conversion will benefit from a roof fan—because warm air rises, attic conversions will naturally be warmer than the rest of the house. A detached garage conversion can't reasonably be linked to the home's HVAC system, and will require a standalone solution.

Where the capacity of the system will allow it, linking to existing HVAC is preferable. In the vast majority of homes, that system will be forced air. A forced-air system is very simple and efficient. The furnace warms air that is distributed through a main supply duct and then out through branch ducts. A cold-air-return duct brings cool air back to the furnace to be heated. If the home has central air-conditioning, it will run through the same ducts, but the flow will be reversed. Tying the addition to a forced air system is usually just a case of running a branch duct into the main duct.

In older homes, the addition may need to connect to a hot water system in which hot water is routed from a boiler through radiators or baseboard units. The plumbing and the pipes are run in the same manner as water supply pipes.

Baseboard heaters are a good choice for additions that can't tie into the home's heating system. For best results, place them along exterior walls and under windows, and keep the space in front of the heater clear of any obstructions.

If your existing HVAC system can't accommodate the added burden of the new space, you'll have to either install a localized, standalone system or upgrade your current system. If you're installing an independent system, you'll find several to choose from:

Radiant heat. The two basic types of radiant heat are hydronic, which produces heat from hot water running through plastic PEX tubing under the subflooring or secured in a slab floor, and electric radiant heat, which is produced by electric mats or cables laid under the finished flooring. These are controlled by thermostats hardwired into a dedicated electrical circuit.

Electric baseboard heat. Produced from standalone electrical units, electric heaters can be wired into a circuit—as with baseboard heaters, or plugged in, as with independent room heaters. Although effective for heating smaller spaces or those that only need to be heated occasionally, these type of heaters can become expensive to use in larger spaces or in colder climates.

Room air conditioners. Where central AC is not practical, install room air conditioners in a wall sleeve (prefabricated metal sleeves are available in different sizes and can easily be framed into an addition's wall) or window. The advantage of these is that you can purchase a unit rated for precisely the addition's square footage. For guidelines on the size of unit required for your space, contact the Association of Home Appliance Manufacturers (AHAM). The latest generation of units are far more energy efficient and quieter than previous models.

A room air conditioner may be installed to cool an addition that is physically removed from the house's main HVAC system or will overtax the cooling capacity of the central air system. Instead of installing the air conditioner in a window, however, preserve your sightlines and improve security by installing the unit in a wall-mounted sleeve.

How to Add Ducts to a Forced Air System

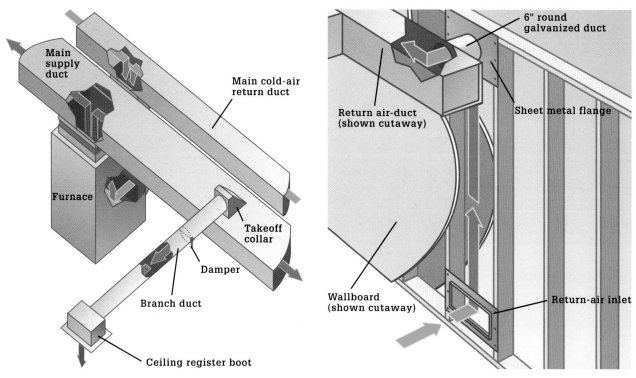

Tying into a forced air ductwork system is usually easiest to do in the basement if the existing ductwork runs in open floor joists. Once you've tapped into the main supply duct you can run ductwork to outlet vents at ceiling level in the basement, or direct the ductwork to an upper level through the walls.

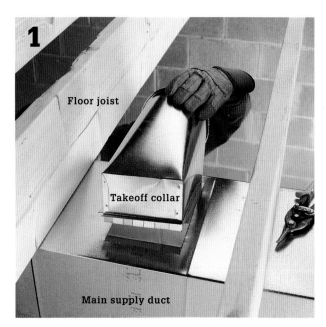

Mount a "takeoff" collar to the top or side of the main duct. Use aviation snips to cut into the main duct, so that tabbed end of the collar can be inserted. Fit the collar into the hole and secure by bending over the tabs inside the duct. Secure two of the tabs with self-tapping sheet metal screws.

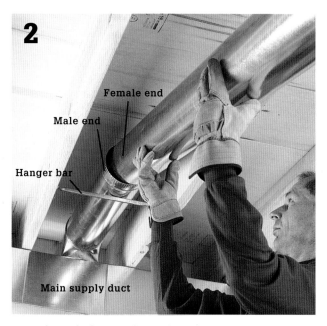

Run a branch duct to the register boot. Starting from the main duct, install sections of ducting by securing female ends over crimped male ends (crimped ends should point away from the main duct). Use hanger bars or straps to support the sections as you work. Fasten the sections together with two self-tapping sheet metal screws.

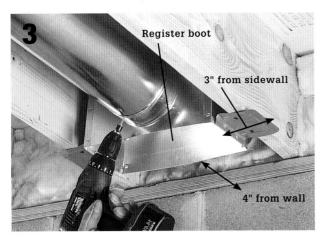

3

Register boot

3" from sidewall

4" from wall

Install the register boot and attach the final duct section. Mount the boot to joists, in position so that the long side is at least 4" from the room's long wall, and short side is at least 3" from any side wall. Install permanent hanger bars or straps every 4 ft. to 6 ft. along the duct.

Efficient Ducting ▸

- Plan duct runs with as few turns as possible, to ensure efficient airflow.
- Round, galvanized metal duct is best—use flexible ducting only where absolutely necessary to continue a run. Consider shallow rectangular ducting where it's necessary to fit between joists and studs.
- Position supply registers near exterior walls, below or above windows. Place return air inlets on walls opposite the supply registers.
- The easiest way to plan a branch duct for an addition is to copy the size and dimensions of existing branch ducts—especially those that serve comparable rooms or spaces.

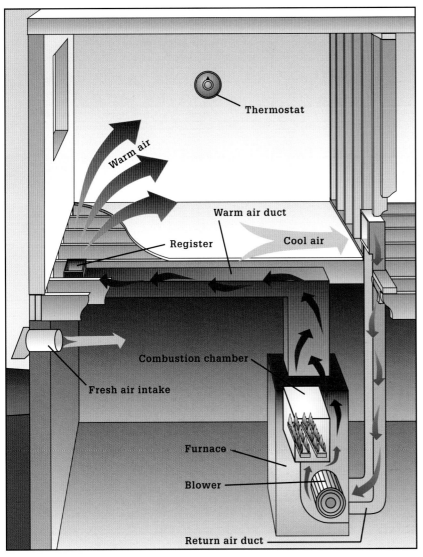

Thermostat

Warm air

Warm air duct

Register

Cool air

Fresh air intake

Combustion chamber

Furnace

Blower

Return air duct

A forced-air system feeds branch ducts via a main supply duct, and dampers allow individual spaces to be unheated when not in use. Warm air registers in additions are preferably located in the floor, but can be run through the ceiling to accommodate the shortest and simplest branch duct route. Cold air return ducts consist of enclosed stud cavities with air inlet at one end and a fitting at the other, feeding into the return air duct. To ensure proper airflow, the cavity should be open, without plumbing or blocking that might restrict air movement, and should be well-sealed to avoid pulling air from elsewhere in the house.

Insulating the Addition

Insulation is essential to minimizing the impact the addition will have on a home's energy bill and ensuring a comfortable living space in all kinds of weather. The key measure of the insulation is the R-value, which represents the insulation's resistance to heat flow. The greater the R-value, the better. Your local codes mandate minimum R-value requirements; in general, exterior walls should be insulated to between R-13 and R-21, which will require 2 × 6 wall framing for most insulation types. Roofs or ceilings are usually insulated to a value of between R-30 and R-38.

R-value is a universal measurement that applies to all types of insulation. Fiberglass batts are the most common among DIYers, but the type you choose will depend on how your addition is constructed, where it's located, and your budget. Batts and blow-in cellulose insulation require a vapor barrier. Install vapor barriers (6 mil plastic sheeting is a common material) to prevent the transfer of moisture from the warm to the cool side and the subsequent damage that moisture can cause.

In parts of the country where the winter is fairly cold, the vapor barrier is placed on the interior side. In locations where warm, humid weather is the norm, the barrier is placed on the exterior side of the insulation. Some types of insulation come "faced," or covered on one side with a vapor barrier attached by the manufacturer. Others, such as sprayed, expanding foam (known as FIP for Foamed in Place) and certain types of polystyrene panels create their own moisture seal and thus don't require a vapor barrier. Use foam or rigid insulation in basements where moisture might be a problem. As always, ask your local building department for requirements in your area.

Insulate the walls and ceiling of a room addition or garage conversion. If your addition is located above an unheated crawlspace or basement, insulate the floor. You can also insulate the interior walls separating an addition from the rest of the house if the addition is heated and cooled locally, or if you want to reduce sound transfer between the two spaces.

Insulation that meets minimum R-value standards is required in exterior walls, ceilings next to unheated roofs, and on floors built over unheated spaces. Encapsulated fiberglass batt insulation is being installed in this basement conversion.

Common Insulation Types ▸

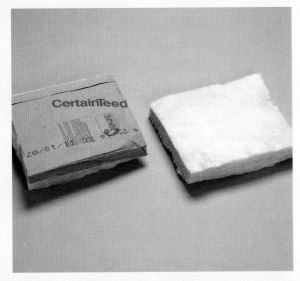

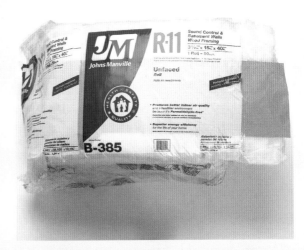

Blankets and batts: Batts are pre-cut panels in standard widths and lengths to fit inside studs spaced 16" or 24" on center, and walls 8 ft. or 9 ft. high. Some manufacturers offer batts with vertical seams that make tearing the batts to fit much easier. Blankets are rolls of insulation that are more efficient when you need to fill long spaces. Both styles are available in fiberglass, spun mineral wool, recycled plastic, and natural fibers. Fiberglass batts are the most common and least expensive type, and are lightweight and easy to work with. Blankets and batts come faced or unfaced, in a wide range of R-values.

Loose fill: As the name implies, this is particulate insulation that is blown into walls and other spaces. Fiberglass and mineral wool are usually blown in dry, while cellulose insulation—shredded bits of paper and cardboard added to water, flame-retardants, and other chemicals and fillers—may be blown in wet or dry. Loose fill is ideal for tight and unusual spaces that are difficult to insulate with batts. R-values vary depending on how the material is prepared and how it is blown in, and the spraying of loose fill is generally best left to professionals.

Spray foam: A combination of polymer and foaming agent, this insulation is mixed on site by special installers and sprayed into walls, floors and ceilings. The foam expands and solidifies, forming a plastic barrier with millions of air pockets. Foam is more expensive than other types of insulation. But R-values are generally higher and there's no air movement, so overall performance is better. The process is quick, and foam does not need a vapor barrier.

How to Install Fiberglass Batt Insulation

Stuff the batt into the wall or ceiling cavity. Whenever handling fiberglass wear proper safety gear, including respirator, enclosed safety glasses, gloves, and a long-sleeved shirt.

Cut batts to fit, rather than compressing them, which can reduce R-value. Use a sharp utility knife to trim the batt ¼" wider and longer than the space. Use a stud as a straightedge and cutting surface, or measure and cut on the subfloor. Cut the unfaced side on faced batts.

Install polyethelene vapor barrier over unfaced batts by draping it across the entire wall, a few inches over on all sides, and stapling it to framing. Cut around obstructions and seal with vapor barrier tape.

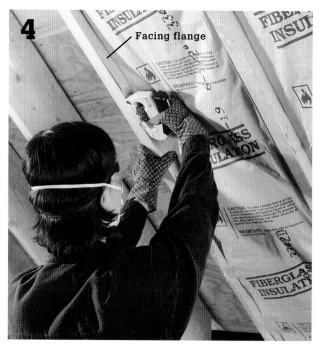

Facing flange

Install faced batts by tucking along the edges so that the flange is flush with the edge of the studs. Staple flanges to the face of framing members, spacing staples every 8". Patch gaps or tears with vapor barrier tape.

How to Insulate a Basement Wall

Insulate the rim joist with strips of 2"-thick isocyanurate rigid insulation with foil facing. Be sure the insulation you purchase is rated for interior exposure (exterior products can produce bad vapors). Use adhesive to bond the insulation to the rim joist, and then caulk around all the edges.

Seal and insulate the top of the foundation wall, if it is exposed, with strips of 1½"-thick, foil-faced isocyanurate insulation. Install the strips using the same type of adhesive and caulk you used for the rim joist insulation.

Attach sheets of 2"-thick polystyrene insulation to the wall from the floor to the top of the wall. Make sure to clean the wall thoroughly and let it dry completely before installing the insulation.

Seal the gaps between the insulation boards with insulation vapor barrier tape. Do not caulk gaps between the insulation boards and the floor.

Install a stud wall by fastening the cap plate to the ceiling joists and the sole plate to the floor. If you have space, allow an air channel between the studs and the insulation. Do not install a vapor barrier.

Finishing the Interior

Finishing your newly constructed addition offers the chance for you to bring the space to life by putting skin on the bones of the framing. Installing final surfaces on the walls, ceilings, and floors is more labor-intensive than technical; given ample time and elbow grease, even an inexperienced DIYer will be able to complete the final stages of construction to professional quality standards.

The process of finishing the interior begins with hanging the drywall. Install panels on the ceiling first and then cover the walls. In most cases, drywall should be hung horizontally on the walls, which hides the finished joints more effectively. Drywall is hung across the joists in the ceiling. Once complete, the joints are taped and "mudded" (covered with compound) and then sanded to a smooth finish in preparation for paint.

Finally, trimwork such as base molding, wainscotting, and the casing around doors and windows is installed, the walls and ceiling are painted, and your choice of flooring is put down. After that, you have only to furnish and enjoy the space you envisioned in the first place.

Installing drywall and taping and finishing the walls brings a very gratifying sense of conclusion to your addition project.

How to Install Drywall on a Ceiling

Snap a chalk line perpendicular to the joists, 48⅛" from the starting wall.

Measure to make sure the first panel will break on the center of a joist. If necessary, cut the panel on the end that abuts the side wall so the panel breaks on the next farthest joist. Load the panel onto a rented panel lift, or use a helper, and lift the panel flat against the joists.

Position the panel with the leading edge on the chalk line and the end centered on a joist. Fasten the panel with screws that penetrate at least ¾" into the framing.

After the first row of panels is installed, begin the next row with a half-panel. This ensures that the butted end joints will be staggered between rows.

How to Install Drywall on Walls

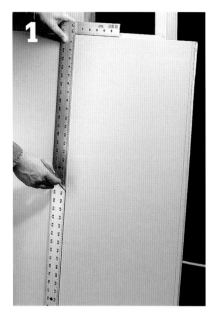

Measure from the wall end or corner to make sure the first panel will break on the center of the stud. If necessary, trim the sheet on the side or end that will be placed in the corner. Mark the stud centers on the panel face and pre-drive screws at each location along the top edge to facilitate fastening. Apply adhesive to the studs.

With a helper or a drywall lifter, hoist the first panel tight against the ceiling, making sure the side edge is centered on a stud. Push the panel flat against the framing and drive the starter screws to secure the panel. Make any cutouts, then fasten the field of the panel.

Measure, cut and install the remaining panels along the upper wall. Bevel panel ends slightly, leaving a 1/8" gap between them at the joint. Butt joints can also be installed using back blocking to create a shallow recess.

Measure, cut and install the bottom row, butting the panels tight to the upper row and leaving a 1/2" gap at the floor. Secure to the framing along the top edge using the starter screws, then make all cutouts before fastening the rest of the panel.

Variation: Drywall can be installed vertically to avoid butt joints, which are more difficult to tape well. However, avoid vertical installation on long, well-lit walls—the seams will show.

How to Tape Drywall Seams

Use a heavy-duty drill with a mixing paddle to thoroughly mix compound to a stiff, yet workable consistency. Use a low speed to avoid whipping air into the compound. Do not overwork setting-type compound, as it will begin to setup. Mix compound occasionally with your taping knife as you work. Clean tools immediately after use.

Apply a thin layer of joint compound to all seams with a 6" drywall knife. Then embed a strip of drywall tape in the compound bed, setting it with the knife and covering it with more compound. Tape corners and cover over screwheads with compound.

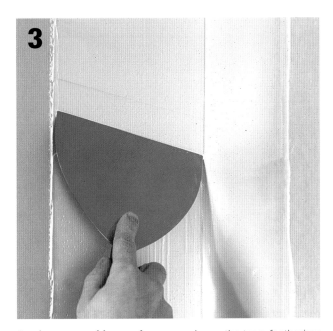

Apply a second layer of compound over the tape, feathering out the edges. When working at inside corners, allow the compound on one wall to dry before you apply compound over the tape on the other wall in the corner.

Spread a final coat of drywall compound over all seams and at all corners, using a 12" taping knife to feather out the edges until they are paper thin. If you do a careful job applying compound you'll only need to do a little bit of light sanding. Use a drywall sanding block with a sanding screen (inset). After all the compound dries, prime the walls with drywall primer and then paint them.

Installing Casing

Stock wood casings provide an attractive border around window and door openings while covering the gaps between the wall surface and the window jamb. Install casings with a consistent reveal between the inside edges of the jambs and the edges of the casings.

In order to fit casings properly, the jambs and wall surfaces must be on the same plane. If one of them protrudes, the casing will not lie flush. To solve this problem, you may need to shave the edges of the jambs down with a block plane. Or you may need to attach jamb extensions to the window or door to match the plane of the wall. For small differences where a drywall surface is too high, you can sometimes use a hammer to compress the drywall around the jambs to allow the casings to lie flush.

Drywall screws rely on the strength of untorn face paper to support the panel. If the paper around the screws becomes torn, drive additional screws nearby where the paper is still intact.

Tools & Materials ▶

Tape measure
Drill
Pencil
Nail set
Hammer or
    pneumatic nailer
Level
Combination square

Straightedge
Miter saw
Casing material
Baseboard molding
    and corner blocks
    (optional)
4d and 6d finish nails
Wood putty
Eye protection

Simple case molding installed with mitered corners is a very common approach to trimming windows and doors. While it lacks visual interest, it is easy to install and relatively inexpensive.

How to Install Mitered Casing on Windows & Doors

On each jamb, mark a reveal line ³⁄₁₆"
to ¼" from the inside edge. The casings
will be installed flush with these lines.

Place a length of casing along one
side jamb, flush with the reveal line.
At the top and bottom of the molding,
mark the points where horizontal
and vertical reveal lines meet. (When
working with doors, mark the molding at
the top only.)

Make 45° miter cuts on the ends
of the moldings. Measure and cut the
other vertical molding piece, using the
same method.

Drill pilot holes spaced every 12"
to prevent splitting, and attach the
vertical casings with 4d finish nails
driven through the casings and into
the jambs. Drive 6d finish nails into the
framing members near the outside edge
of the casings.

Measure the distance between the
side casings and cut top and bottom
casings to fit, with ends mitered at
45°. If the window or door unit is not
perfectly square, make test cuts on
scrap pieces to find the correct angle
of the joints. Drill pilot holes and attach
with 4d and 6d finish nails.

Locknail the corner joints by drilling
pilot holes and driving 4d finish nails
through each corner, as shown. Drive
all nail heads below the wood surface
using a nail set, then fill the nail holes
with wood putty.

Choosing Floorcoverings

The flooring for an addition is most often matched to the flooring in the adjoining area or in similar rooms in the house. Wood floors can be matched to the existing floor by carefully selecting woods and stains. Carpet may be more difficult to match because carpet colors can change over time. Where a close match cannot be made, carpet and wood floors are excellent complements to one another. If the addition is an extension of a kitchen, or the home is a style that incorporates tile floors, a complementary tile floor will help the addition blend in.

Wood: Natural hard- or softwood floors are distinctive, long-lasting, and feel comfortable underfoot in warm and cool weather. Plank or board wood floors are, however, expensive to buy and complex to install. Laminate wood, also known as engineered wood flooring, is a less-expensive version made of wood plies glued together and topped by a finished surface. If the existing home has wood floors, matching them is the best way to make a fluid interior transition. Match the style—width of planks or boards and type of wood—and the finish of the floors, to make the transition seamless.

Laminate Flooring: Comprised of a dense fiber base covered by a photographic layer topped with a protective coating, laminate flooring is available in an amazing array of very realistic faux finishes, from a full range of wood grains, to stone and even ceramic tile surface appearances. Laminate floors such as Pergo are easy to install and are often laid as "floating" floors, with individual units snapped together over a pad that is laid over the subfloor. Laminate floors are a cost-effective alternative to matching existing flooring exactly.

Carpet: Color is one of many different factors you'll need to consider, whether you're looking to match existing carpet in the house or just want to buy a nice warm floor covering for your new space. Carpet fibers determine look and wear properties and there are several different fiber materials, all with their own properties. The number of fibers per inch, and the "twist" of the fiber can affect the surface appearance. But the most influential factor in how a carpet looks is the pile. Basically, the fibers are looped through the carpet base and either cut, left as loops, or a combination of both. In addition, the fibers—whether looped or cut—may be different heights over the area of the carpet. Generally, the more expensive the carpet, the more durable and resistant to fading and staining the carpet will be. But test samples with your hand and, preferably, with your foot to see how it feels and if the pile rebounds or shows marks. Carpet installation is best left to professionals because it requires expertise to install without showing seams or wrinkles.

Tile Floors: Traditional ceramic or terra cotta tiles are available in a range of finishes and standardized sizes, and tile is fairly easy to install. However, hard tiles aren't appropriate for every home and they do not complement many traditional home floors such as oak floors. However, for an easy tile option, turn to carpet and wood tiles as simple alternatives to more traditional forms. Newer styles of carpet tiles are available in high-end designs that allow great flexibility in creating interesting patterns.

Attic Conversions

U nfinished attics are hidden gems in the floorplan of a house. Although they are less common in newer homes, attics represent a readymade alternative to a bumpout or room addition. While converting existing space doesn't offer the flexibility of building from scratch, an attic can be turned into an airy living space, workspace, or playspace. And an attic conversion can be accomplished for a fraction of the cost of adding a similar new space onto the house.

These spaces are best suited for certain types of rooms, including bedrooms, home offices, and hobby rooms. Larger attics make perfect rec rooms or master bedroom suites. Generally, however, any room that requires plumbing, such as a kitchen or bathroom, is better left to lower floors where it is less of a challenge to run new plumbing. A third-floor attic can also stress the water pressure in some houses, resulting in low water flow.

Regardless of what type of room you put there, converting an attic will require some basic modifications. But with a modest amount of work, you can convert that unused space into valuable square footage.

In this chapter:

- Planning an Attic Conversion
- Building an Attic Addition Floor
- Concealing Utilities
- Building an Attic Staircase
- Building an Attic Dormer
- Building an Attic Kneewall With Recessed Storage
- Attic Addition Ceilings

Planning an Attic Conversion

Converting an attic into a fabulous room with a view entails the same sort of planning that creating a new room from scratch requires. The difference is that your plans must account for the increased load a living space imposes upon a structure that already exists. This puts an added emphasis on your preliminary evaluation, and means the conversion may involve significant modification of the structure and systems already in place.

The most important considerations in planning your attic conversion are access, headroom, wall and floor support, air circulation, and lighting. Because many attics are not specifically designed to accommodate the stress and loads of a built-out living space, the first step is to assess the current state of the space. A thorough examination is essential to understanding the scope and complexity of the structural and mechanical changes you'll need to make.

Roof structure. If your roof is supported with trusses, you'll see interconnected webs and chords crisscrossing the space. These supports don't allow for a living space, and removing or altering them is a complicated, risky undertaking requiring expert engineering skills. Look for another location for your addition if trusses form the roof structure. If your roof is supported with traditional rafters, you'll have much more usable attic space to work with. If your rafters are connected with collar ties that block headroom, the ties probably can be moved higher or perhaps even removed entirely—consult a structural engineer.

Smaller-than-normal rafters may be supported by horizontal boards called purlins. These run the length of the attic, perpendicular to the rafters, and are supported by diagonal members called struts. Purlins and struts can be replaced with a more useful kneewall. If the cavity between rafters is not deep enough to hold enough insulation to meet minimum R-values required by code, attach 1 × 2 or 2 × 2 nailers to the rafter edges to deepen the bays.

The type of roof framing in your house informs the viability of any attic conversion. Standard rafter framing (left) creates a large open area with sufficient headroom for use as a living space. Roof trusses (right) have certain advantages over rafters when building, but they make an expansion of any practical size virtually impossible.

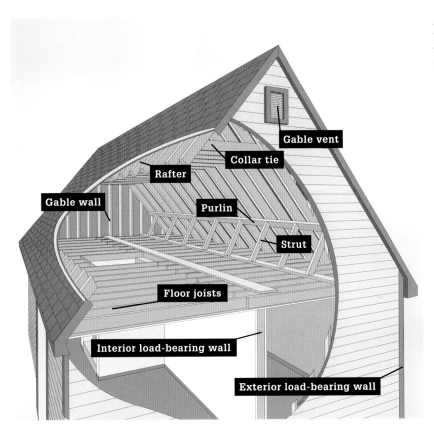

Gable vent

Collar tie

Rafter

Gable wall

Purlin

Strut

Floor joists

Interior load-bearing wall

Exterior load-bearing wall

Floor structure. The floor joists in your attic need to support the total load of the living space, but joists in many attics originally were not designed to accommodate that much weight. Consequently, the joists may need to be reinforced with "sister" joists, which are members that are face-nailed to the existing joists to increase their load-bearing capacity.

The amount of load that an attic floor can support safely increases dramatically if there are load-bearing columns or walls below. Check for the number and size of load-bearing supports—they will usually run perpendicular to the joists and will themselves be supported all the way to the foundation. Load-bearing walls or columns may need to be reinforced to support increased load.

Headroom Requirements ▶

Building codes are very clear on the headroom required to turn an attic into a living space. The final space as planned must be a minimum of 70 sq. ft. total, with at least 7 ft. of free space in any one direction. More importantly, 50 percent of the "usable floor space" must have a floor-to-ceiling height of at least 7½ ft. For code purposes, the term usable floor space refers to all the area in the attic with at least 5 ft. of clearance from floor to ceiling. If your attic as is does not meet these requirements, you can make modifications, such as adding a dormer, which will increase headroom over the same floor space area.

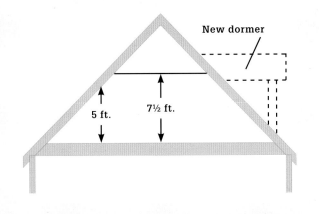

New dormer

5 ft.

7½ ft.

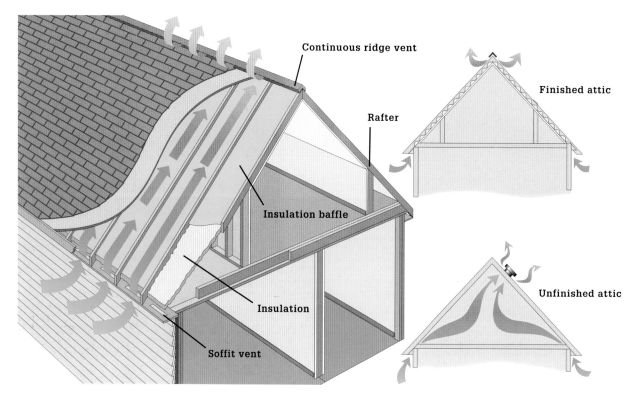

Continuous ridge vent

Finished attic

Rafter

Insulation baffle

Insulation

Unfinished attic

Soffit vent

A roof ventilation system works in conjunction with attic insulation: Insulation forms a thermal barrier that keeps in the home's conditioned air, while the ventilation system uses outdoor air to keep the roof deck cool and dry. In most unfinished attics, the entire attic space is ventilated, and proper air flow can be achieved with roof vents or gable-wall vents.

Roof ventilation. Roof vents allow the free flow of air from intakes to exhaust or outtake vents. The air intake vents are usually in the soffits and the outtake vents are in the top of the gable and in or near the roof ridge. Make sure that your construction plans leave a channel for airflow between intake and outtake vents. In addition to ensuring the roof can "breathe," you'll need to provide airflow inside the finished space, which is usually done with one or more windows, perhaps in addition to an operable skylight or roof window. Roof vents can be powered (electric or solar) to increase the pull and, therefore, the amount of air circulated over a given period of time. Vents come in a wide range of sizes and capacities, and include mushroom or box types that are installed over one or more rafter bays, continuous ridge vents that run along the span of the roof's ridge, and gable wall vents placed on the vertical surface near the peak of the roof.

Baffles ▸

To maintain airflow in a finished attic space, you'll need to leave at least an inch-deep buffer of open space between the roof sheathing and the attic insulation. This is done by installing plastic channels, called baffles, between rafters prior to installing the insulation. You may also need to install baffles at the base of rafter bays to prevent blocking intake vents.

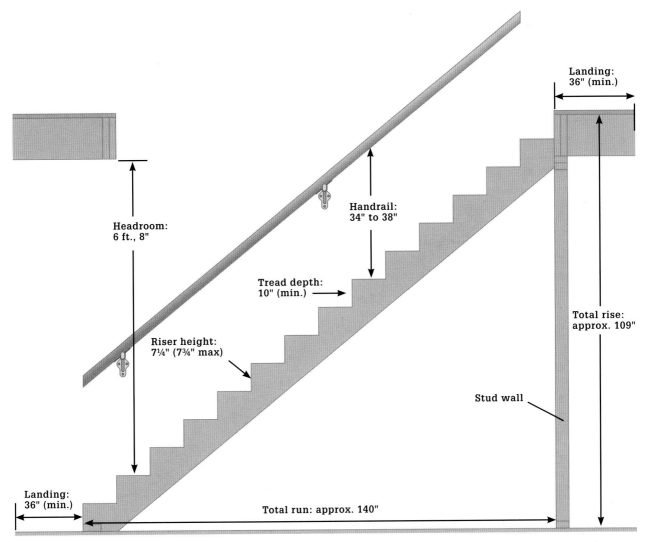

Stairway code requirements typically call for a 36"-wide stairway with 6 ft., 8" of headroom and uniform treads and risers. The ends of staircases are anchored to a cleat at the bottom and doubled floor joists at the top.

Access. In addition to headroom (see page 181), access concerns the entry and exit points to the addition. Creating an actual entrance and exit for the space, if suitable access doesn't already exist, depends on how the house is arranged and on local building and fire codes. In most cases, you'll need to install a new staircase that's at least 36" wide with landings at the top and bottom that are 36" wide as well. Some codes call for a means of egress, such as a fire escape or egress window, that is separate from the staircase.

Lighting. Lighting is a related issue to ventilation, in that both can be resolved by installing new windows or skylights. Wherever possible, your addition plan should include openings to allow for daylight at different times during the day. In determining the position of those openings, you should also consider the view they'll provide.

Mechanicals. Mechanical services are as important in the attic as they are in any other addition. There may already be an electrical circuit serving the attic, in which case you'll probably tie into the circuit to run wiring for lighting fixtures and outlets. If your attic conversion is more complicated, it may require running a whole new circuit from the breaker box up through the walls to the attic. In addition, more involved conversions can include a bathroom or other plumbed feature. Plumbing an attic conversion must be done very carefully because even the smallest leak has the potential to cause excessive damage to the structure and the floors below. Generally, plumbing and wiring an attic conversion are best left to professionals. See pages 156–159 for a wiring plan for an attic conversion.

Building an Attic Addition Floor

In most homes, the attic floor was designed as a ceiling, not a floor. Structurally the difference is significant; a ceiling needs to support far less weight. This means that you will probably have to reinforce and finish the attic floor to accommodate the conversion to a living space.

Before you begin work on the floor, check your local building codes. They will likely require an engineering assessment of the attic floor's load capacity. Even if your code doesn't require it, an engineering assessment is a good idea because so many other components are dependent on the attic floor structure—not the least of which is occupant safety. Engineers and codes use "load" requirements as baselines for assessing an attic floor. "Dead load" is the weight of building materials. "Live load" is the weight of everything else, including stored boxes, furniture, and occupants. The floors of most unfinished attics have the same live and dead load, usually about 10 pounds per sq. ft. (psf). Most codes require 30 psf live load for an attic used as a living space, and some even require 40 psf. Meeting that requirement is a matter of beefing up the structural system of the floor.

That can be done in one of two ways. The most common method is "sistering," in which a new equal-width joist is attached to each existing joist, essentially doubling the joists' size. Some circumstances preclude sistering: for example, when the existing joists are smaller than 2 × 6, are too far apart (usually 24" or more on center), or where obstacles prevent you from mating new joists to the old. In these cases, a new joist should be added in the spaces between the existing joists.

Tools & Materials ▸

Hammer
Tape measure
Circular saw

Construction adhesive
8d nails
2 × 8s

Attic joists typically rest on top of exterior walls and on an interior load-bearing wall, where they overlap from side to side and are nailed together. *Note: Working on an unfinished attic floor presents a physical danger as well as the potential for structural damage. Always work on a sheet of plywood set atop the joists. This platform will prevent any missteps and offers a stable base from which to hammer or position framing members.*

How to Reinforce Attic Floor Joists

Prepare and measure for new joists. Remove insulation, blocking, and wiring from between the existing joists. Measure the length of each joist and cut a sister joist to the same length. Bevel-cut the tops of the joist ends if necessary to fit under the roof sheathing. Joists that do not run full width should overlap at load-bearing walls or girders: check your local building codes for minimum overlap requirements.

Check each joist for a "crown"—an arch along its length—by sighting down both edges of each joist. Mark the crown; joists must be installed "crown-up." Cut the board to length.

Coat the face of each existing joist with construction adhesive and set the sister joist into place, snug against the existing joist. Toenail the sister joist to the top plates of both supporting walls.

Face-nail the sistered joist to the existing joist. Nail three nails in a row, and space rows 12" to 16" apart. Install blocking between joists as required by local code.

How to Construct a New Attic Floor

1

Remove any blocking or metal or wood bridging between joists. Cut 2 × 4 spacers to fit tightly between joists. Lay the spacers flat against the top plates of all supporting walls, and nail them in place.

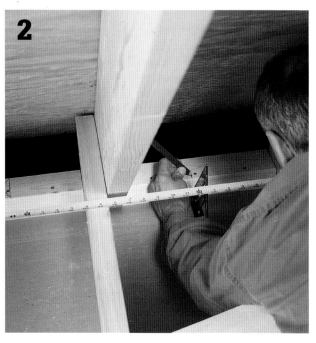

2

Carefully measure the tops of existing joists and use a speed square to transfer measurements down onto spacers. Mark new rafter layout 16" on center along one exterior wall. Make the same marks on any interior load bearing wall, and mark layout on the opposite exterior wall offset by 1½" to account for joist overlap at the interior wall.

3

Determine the new joist length by measuring from one outside wall to the other side of the interior wall. Measure, mark, and cut the outside edge of the new joist to accommodate the slope of the roof sheathing.

4

Set the joists in place on their layout marks, making sure the crown for each joist is up. Position joists snug against the roof sheathing on the outside edge. Toenail the outside end of each joist to the spacer on the exterior wall.

Apply construction adhesive to the faces where the joists overlap. Face-nail overlapping joists together at the interior wall. Use at least six nails in at least three rows to secure the joists together.

Nail blocking or bridges between the joists as required by local code. At the very least, block the new joists as close as possible to their outside ends, and where they overlap.

Installing the Subfloor

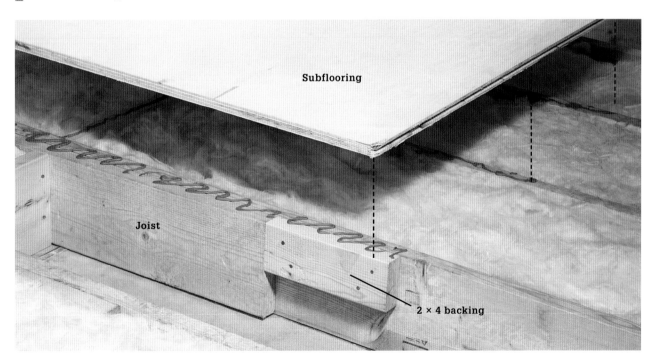

Subflooring

Joist

2 × 4 backing

The subfloor is installed after the new floor framing is finished, mechanical services have been installed, and the floor joist cavities are insulated. Once the floor has been inspected by the building inspector, secure the tongue-in-groove plywood floor panels to the joists with construction adhesive and deck screws. The sheets should be laid perpendicular to the joists and the end joints staggered between rows. Where the joists overlap, add backing blocks as needed to provide nailing surfaces for the sheets. Nail a 2 × 4 scrap to the face of each joist to support the edges of the intervening sheets.

Concealing Utilities

Soffits and chases are framed structures used to conceal pipes, electrical fixtures such as lights and fans, and ductwork in newly finished spaces. Soffits are rarely used in a converted attic because the ceiling is either left peaked following the slope of the rafters, or a flat ceiling is built, which itself can conceal any overhead fixtures. But chases can be useful in framing vertical pipes or ducts that run directly through the space.

Soffits and chases are framed roughly the same way, although a soffit is meant to be hung from joists and a chase is framed vertically. A frame is created with 2 × 2s for short columns around small pipes, or 2 × 4s framing a box around a large pipe such as a soil stack. The top and bottom plates of the chase are created with simple butt joints and nailed to the rafters and subfloor respectively. Use the rafters to mark the studs, and cut them to length—minus the combined width of the lumber used in the top and bottom plates, and mitered to fit the angle of the rafters. Prevent noise by insulating around the pipe before installing the drywall on the chase.

A soffit is a bump-out that drops down from the ceiling to conceal ductwork, recessed light fixtures and other obstructions.

Variations for Building Soffits

2 × 2 soffit: Build two ladder-like frames for the soffit sides using standard 2 × 2s. Install braces every 16 or 24" to provide nailing support for the edges of the drywall. Attach the side frames to the joists on either side of the obstruction using nails or screws. Then, install crosspieces beneath the obstacle, tying the two sides together.

Simple steel-frame soffit: With ½" drywall, this construction works for soffits up to 16" wide; with ⅝" drywall, up to 24" wide. Use 1⅝, 2½, or 3⅝" steel studs and tracks. Fasten a track to the ceiling and a stud to the adjoining wall using drywall screws. Cut a strip of drywall to form the side of the soffit, and attach a steel stud flush with the bottom edge of the strip using Type S screws. Attach the assembly to the ceiling track, then cut and install drywall panels to form the soffit bottom.

Steel-frame soffit with braces: Use 1⅝, 2½, or 3⅝" steel studs and tracks. Fasten a track to the ceiling and wall with drywall screws. Cut studs to form the side and bottom of the soffit, fasten them to the tracks every 16 or 24" on-center using Type S panhead screws, then join the pieces with metal angle (you can use a steel track cut in half lengthwise). Use a string line and locking clamps to help keep the frame straight and square during construction.

Building an Attic Staircase

Converting an attic into livable space requires a code-compliant point of access. Where building codes and basic comfort are concerned, that means a permanent set of stairs. The stair-building techniques described here are applicable to stairs in any kind of addition, whether it's a garage with a loft, or a room addition that requires exterior stairs leading from an exterior door at the top of a tall foundation down to the backyard. No matter the application, the key to building safe and comfortable stairs is all about the numbers—from the appropriate ratio of stair depth to height, to the required headroom.

An attic staircase must be at least 36 inches wide, and the overall footprint of a common straight-run staircase can consume 40 to 50 square feet. The top of the stairs must open into a space with adequate headroom—at least 7 feet 6 inches—and landings must be at least 36 inches wide and 36 inches deep. Most codes also require the staircase steps, measured from the nose of the tread, have at least 80 inches of headroom. A handrail is necessary if there are more than two steps. These requirements are restrictive enough to preclude running the staircase in most hallways. So where should you build your steps? Good potential locations include large closets, small unused bedrooms, and next to the wall in a large room.

To accommodate tight space constraints, many attic access stairs are built with a different configuration than the straight-run design.

Creating a staircase to your attic conversion often requires a fair amount of creativity and extremely efficient usage of space.

Staircase Math ▸

Once you figure out where the staircase will go, you need to run the numbers required for building it. The two numbers that form the basis for any stairs are "rise" and "run." Total rise is the height of the staircase from its footing to the top of the top platform; total run is the depth of the staircase from the front of the first step to the front of the top platform. Unit rise and unit run are the measures defining each step. Unit rise is the height of the "riser," the vertical piece separating treads. Unit run is the depth of each tread. These should be exactly uniform over the span of the stairs.

Stair measurements have long been standardized to create a comfortable and safe ratio of rise to run. Codes reflect this knowledge—treads must be at least 10" deep with at least a 1" "nosing." Risers must be at least

7" and no more than 7¾" high, but are ideally between 7¼" and 7¾". A common formula builders use is that the combination of two risers and one tread should always equal between 24" and 26". Determine the number of risers needed by dividing total finish rise by 7.5 (round up if necessary). Then divide that number into the total finish rise to get the actual height of each riser. The number of treads will be one less than the number of risers. The total run will be that number times 10 inches per tread. To avoid errors, draw a scaled sideview of the stairs on graph paper, including finished floors at the top and bottom. Once you have the actual rise and run measurements, you can begin marking and cutting the three stringers, or main supports for the stairs. You'll find specialty rise-and-run calculators for free online, and for sale in home centers.

Definitions of Stairway Terms ▸

Landing: A landing is a flat surface at the top and bottom of a stairway, or it may also occur at points within a stairway. A landing must be at least as wide as the stairway and at least 36 inches deep.

Nosing: A tread nose (nosing) is the part of a horizontal stair surface that projects outward beyond a solid (closed) riser below.

Riser: A riser is the vertical part of a stair. A closed riser is created with solid material between adjacent treads. An open riser has no material (except for any required guards) between adjacent treads.

Stairway (flight of stairs): A series of risers and treads that is not interrupted by a landing. A flight of stairs includes the landings at the top and bottom of the flight. A stairway with only a top and bottom landing has one flight of stairs. A stairway with a landing in the middle has two flights of stairs.

Tread: A tread is the horizontal part of a stair. A tread is sometimes called the step.

Winder tread: A winder is a tread with one end wider than the other. Winders are often used at intermediate landings to change a stairway's direction.

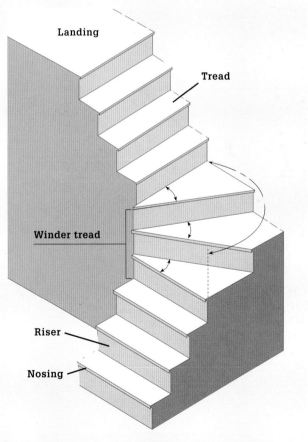

Stairway components include: tread, winder tread, nosing, riser, landing, flight of stairs.

▌Typical Layouts

L-SHAPED STAIR

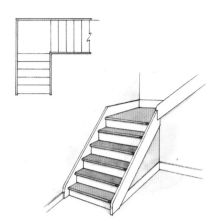

STRAIGHT STAIR WITH OPEN RISERS

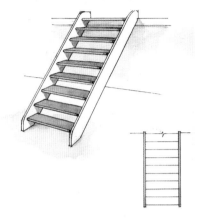

STANDARD SWITCHBACK STAIR

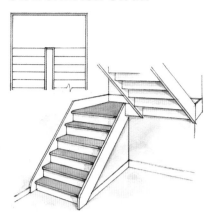

STRAIGHT STAIR

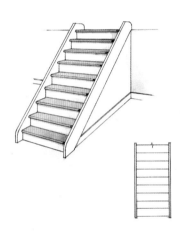

SWITCHBACK STAIR WITH WINDERS

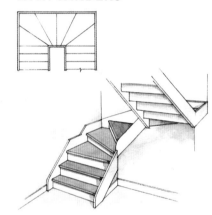

SWITCHBACK STAIR WITH INTERMEDIATE FLIGHT

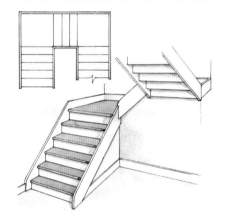

SIDE-FLIGHT STAIR

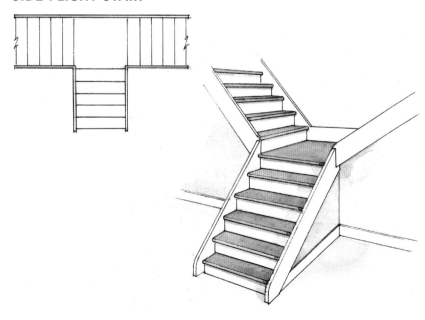

Depending on where they are located in a space, stairs can be freestanding (with no walls on either side) open on one side, or entirely enclosed by walls. As you will see, there are dozens of variations on these common types.

Tips for Designing Stairs

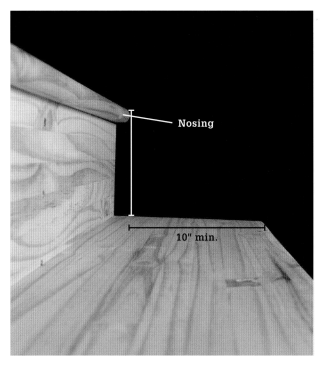

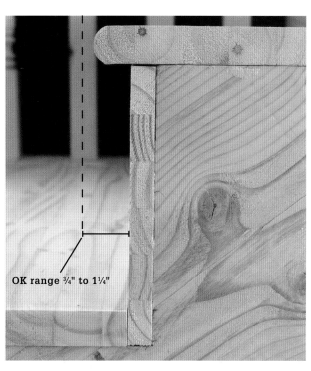

Provide a tread depth of at least 10" if treads have a nosing or at least 11" if treads have no nosing.

Provide a tread nosing depth of at least ¾" and not more than 1¼". Do not exceed ⁹⁄₁₆" radius for a curved nosing or ½" depth for a beveled nosing.

Install a light switch at the top and bottom of stairways with at least six risers.

Size your riser height to account for the thickness of floor covering materials to avoid exceeding riser height and riser difference limits.

How to Frame a Staircase Opening

Measure and mark the new opening dimensions on the ceiling of the space below the attic. Cut the ceiling drywall along the marks with a drywall saw and remove the drywall.

Transfer the opening dimensions to the tops of the attic joists. Recheck measurements and then snap chalk lines to show where joists are to be cut.

Cut and remove joists, with a helper supporting the cut sections from below. You'll use the cut sections to make the double headers for the opening.

Attach sister joists to the existing joists at the sides of the opening, using construction adhesive and 10d common nails in rows of three, spaced at 12" intervals. Drive nails from both sides if you have access.

Cut headers to size and make double headers by joining with nails and construction adhesive. Nail joist hangers on either end of double header.

Butt the side of the double headers against the cut "tail" joists and nail headers into place on trimmer joists. Slip joist hangers onto the ends of the tail joists and nail them to the double headers.

Spiral Staircases ▸

A spiral staircase can be installed to create access to the attic where a traditional staircase won't fit. As long as minimum widths and headroom clearance are met, most building codes will allow the use of a spiral staircase. Classic metal staircases can be ordered in easy-to-assemble kits.

How to Build Straight-Run Stairs

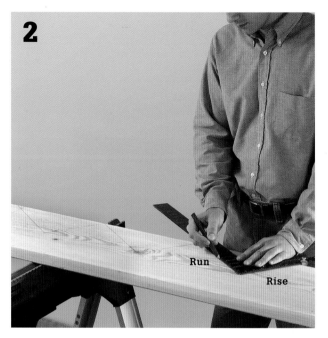

Transfer the location of the upper landing end to the floor below, using a plumb bob. Measure and mark the front of the run. If the stairs will be attached to the wall at one side, outline the layout of the undercarriage structure onto the wall.

Begin marking cuts on a 2 × 10 stringer by positioning framing square with "unit-run" measurement intersecting the top edge near the bottom end of the stringer, and unit rise intersecting the top edge on the top end. The stringer should be construction grade lumber rated B or better.

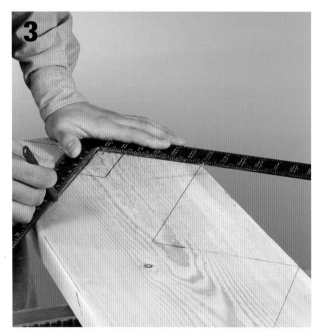

Continue marking the first unit-run lines at the bottom edge of the stringer board. Mark the cut for the floor end of the stringer. Also mark cutouts for a 2 × 4 kickboard. Lay out the remaining unit-run and unit-rise lines on the stringer. Extend the last unit-rise line down to the lower edge of the board, to mark the spot where the stringer attaches to the header.

Make the cutouts in the stringer. Use a circular saw for the straight cuts, but stop cutting before the blade reaches the crotch of each cutout. Finish the cutouts with a jigsaw or hand saw.

5

Test-fit the first stringer in place, checking plumb of rise and level of run. Hold it against the wall if that is where it will be installed. When you've determined that it fits, use the first stringer as a template to mark the remaining two stringers. Align and clamp the boards before marking, and use a sharp pencil. Cut the other stringers.

6

Position the kickboard correctly and fasten it to the floor. Place the outside stringers in position and secure them to the header using metal hangers nailed on the inside of the stringers.

7

Position the center "carriage" stringer at the top of the stair opening and check across the tread runs to make sure they are level. Nail the carriage to hangers on the header. If the inside stringer runs along wall, secure it to the wall studs with lag screws.

8

Drill countersunk pilot holes, and then screw or finish nail the riser boards to the stringers. Do the same with the treads. Spread construction glue on the stringers to cut down on future squeaks.

How to Install Staircase Handrails

Measure and mark the peg holes for the balusters. Drill the holes and install the balusters, applying the glue directly to the dowel end or into the peg holes.

Position the newel post at the bottom of the staircase and drill holes for the four L brackets. Screw L brackets to the floor, and then to the base of the newel post, and cover with concealing trim nailed in place with finishing nails. *Note: The manufacturer may recommend a different method for attaching the newel post to the floor.*

Glue the underside of the handrail to the tops of balusters, and drill a small pilot hole for screws at an angle through the baluster into handrail. Drill holes for the newel mounting bracket and screw the handrail to the newel post. Plug the screwholes before finishing stairs.

If the stairs run against a wall, use a wall-mounted handrail on the wall side. Screw mounting brackets evenly spaced along the staircase, and screw the handrail to the mounting brackets.

Finishing Attic Stairs

Once your staircase is constructed, you can leave it as is and simply carpet the surface of the stairs, or paint or stain the entire structure. You can also choose among the different ways to enclose the open space underneath the staircase to create a more complete appearance, or one that better suits your particular space.

Framing the understair area. Use 2 × 4 studs to frame a wall as you would elsewhere, running studs between a sole plate and the stringers. You can simply enclose the framed wall space with drywall or plywood for a box-like finished look, or put a bit more work in and frame in shelves for added storage.

Opt for a more sophisticated look by finishing the wall and framing in a simple door, which will create abundant concealed storage for vacuum cleaners and other essentials. Depending on where the stairs are located, the understair area can also serve as a compact office space, with built-shelves lining the wall over a desk.

Walling in the staircase. In some situations, you may want to partially or fully conceal the staircase. In this case, you can frame and finish a wall on the open side to create a staircase passageway. Even if you are trapping the staircase between two walls, you must still use handrails on each side.

The understair area of an attic staircase offers the chance to be creative. In this case, the homeowner uses the area as a cozy play space for the children in the house, with a decorative piece of canvas cut and painted to conceal the space when children are not at play. *Note: This staircase still needs to be fitted with a grippable handrail to be code compliant.*

Building an Attic Dormer

A dormer can transform an attic space, delivering the three attic essentials of light, ventilation, and headroom with a single alteration. What's more, a dormer helps meet code requirements: most codes require that unrestricted window space equal at least 8 percent of the room's square footage. And with proper positioning and proportion, the right dormer adds immeasurably to the view from the outside, as well as from inside.

All these benefits don't come easy. A dormer is a serious structural alteration to the roof and attic, and constructing one requires significant expertise. Because of the powerful impact a dormer has on the architecture of the entire house, you should always consult with an architect to help you decide on the appropriate size and type of dormer. Although all dormers are perpendicular projections breaking the plane of the existing roofline, there are actually many different types of dormers. All are, however, variations of two styles: a gable or a shed.

The styles relate to the type of roof on the dormer. In a gable dormer, the roof is peaked, just as with a house. Gable dormers are most appropriate for homes with severe roof slopes and those with complex roof lines. Shed dormers have flat roofs, making them easier to build. They are usually used where the roof slope is less acute and the architecture is fairly simple. Either style of dormer may be built flush with the roof edge, so that the bottom front edge of the dormer is the same as the edge of the existing roof, or as a "set-back," in which the dormer's front wall is several feet up the slope of the roof from the eaves. A set-back dormer offers increased headroom, but the choice is usually made based on what looks best with the house's architecture.

Building a dormer is a complex process, but the primary goal in planning and executing the construction should be to leave the roof open to the elements for as short a time as possible. In doing this type of construction work, you should use some sort of fall-arresting safety device because much of the work is done on the slope of the roof. The actual work is a combination of basic framing skills and roofing techniques.

Three distinctive dormers feature a distinctive fascia style borrowed from the house, which makes them appear as part of the original construction. The extra headroom and light provided by these three allows the attic to be used as a third floor.

This elaborate attic dormer lets light into the attic conversion and adds a stunning visual element to the exterior of the house.

Dormer Styles

Dormers come in many sizes and shapes because houses come in many architectural styles. The idea is to select the right style and size dormer for your home so that the dormer looks like it's always been a part of the structure and doesn't create an imbalance in the architectural perspective. That's not really difficult given the range of dormer styles available. In addition to the styles described below, most can be designed to "nest" or be inset—meaning they are built with their framework inside the space of the attic. They can also be partially inset or, more commonly, they can be built out, with the framed structure standing entirely above the roof plane. Usually, one type of dormer is most appropriate to your home's architectural style, but a different dormer style may work as well. Never combine dormer styles or you risk creating an unappealing jumble of rooflines that will detract from, rather than add to, the overall appeal of the house.

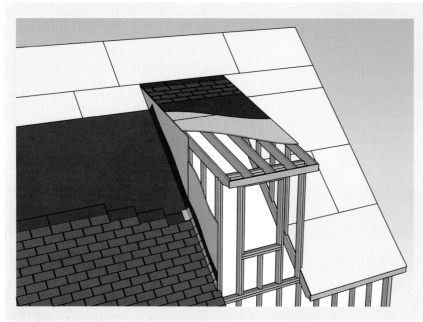

A shed dormer is the easiest style to build and one that is well suited to many different types of home architecture. It's often wisest, when possible, to position the dormer flush with the roof edge rather than set back, because much of the weight of a flush dormer is supported by the exterior load-bearing wall.

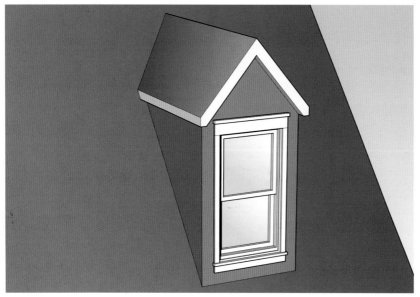

Gable: This is the most basic peaked-roof dormer style. It has a single ridge and a flat gable wall containing a window. The framing of the roof creates interesting angles within the converted attic, adding visual interest. The easiest way to ensure that a gable dormer blends with the existing roof and house structure is to match the pitch of the dormer's roof to that of the existing roof.

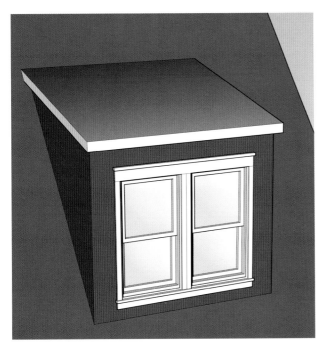

Shed: A simpler version of the gable dormer, a shed dormer features a flat sloped roof that opens up more of the interior space. Because of its basic structure, shed dormers can be easily extended sideways, stretching over a significant—if not the entire—expanse of the roof.

Hip: Hipped dormers are complex, difficult to build, and complement fewer architectural styles than any other dormer. But the sophisticated appearance can add immeasurably to the look of a house, as long as it is in restrained proportion to the rest of the roof's angles and surface area. The interior of a hip dormer is a visually busy collage of angles that enliven the attic space.

Eyebrow: An eyebrow dormer brings a modicum of light and air to the attic space, but adds very little in the way of additional headroom. The modest dimensions of an eyebrow make this more of an architectural ornament than a structural element.

Barrel: Drawing its name from it's arched roof, barrel dormers can provide a sculptural aspect that relieves some of the linear harshness of boxier architectural styles. The shape of the roof on the inside lends a unique aspect to the attic space, evocative of the inside of an old ship.

How to Build a Shed Dormer

Mark cutting lines on the framing members. First, measure the dormer opening outline on the undersides of the rafters. Mark horizontal cuts with a chalk line. Use a torpedo level to mark the plumb cuts on each rafter.

To transfer the location of the cutout corners, hammer long nails up through the roof sheathing at the corner points of the opening. Make sure the nails penetrate up through the sheathing and shingles.

Preventing a Fall ▸

It only takes one tiny misstep when working on a roof to cause serious injury. That's why it makes sense to take appropriate safety precautions when working on a dormer structure from the roof side. One of the most effective safeguards is a "fall-arrest" system. Systems range from a full-body harness with a lifeline connection, to a simpler safety belt attached to a secure anchor by means of a sturdy leash. Most fall-arrest systems can be rented or purchased. But the goal is the same no matter which system you choose—to create a failsafe guard against a sudden and unwanted descent.

3

Frame stud walls according to your plan. Do as much of this work as you can prior to cutting into the roof.

4

Remove roofcoverings in the project area. To mark the project area, snap chalklines connecting the nails that you drove up through the roof deck at the corners. Strip shingles and roofing paper from the area until it is fully clear. Where possible, remove whole shingles rather than cutting shingles.

5

Use the nails as guides to snap a fresh chalkline to mark the top of the opening onto the sheathing. Snap a chalkline for the sides, ¾" outside of the nails.

6

Cut and remove the roof sheathing. On the outside of the roof, use a circular saw set to cut to the thickness of the sheathing. Use a hammer and pry bar from underneath to remove sheathing. Makes sure the area below the roof is clear before you pry off the sheathing.

(continued)

Cut the rafters along the cutting lines, using a reciprocating saw. The cut ends should be perpendicular to the floor.

Cut sister rafters to length and attach them to the outsides of the rafters on the cutout edges. Join the members with construction glue and rows of three nails spaced every 12" and driven through both faces of the doubled rafter.

Nail the new header to the ends of the trimmer rafters, snug against the ends of the cut rafters.

Tip the face wall up into position, over the exterior load-bearing wall. Nail through the soleplate into the joists.

Mark and cut a template rafter, with the appropriate ends cut for the roof slope and bird's mouth cut. Use the template rafter to mark the rest of the rafters, and then cut the rafters.

Install rafters by nailing them to the header and then to the top plate of the face wall. Frame the side walls with 2 × 4 or 2 × 6 studs. Mark the studs for final cutting by holding them plumb along the side, top, and bottom rafters.

Install nailers between the face wall studs at the point where the wall intersects with the existing roof deck. Cut and install rated sheathing panels on the dormer roof and walls. *Note: Add 2 × 4 furring strips to the inside faces of the sidewall studs before insulating and installing wallcovering.*

Finish the exterior and interior as you would finish any other addition project. This should include wrapping the dormer in building wrap, installing the window, installing flashing along the front and sides of the dormer, then adding siding to match the house siding. Shingle the roof, interweaving new shingles along the joint with the existing roof. Paint exposed rafters or install soffits, fascia, and gutters.

Building an Attic Kneewall With Recessed Storage

A kneewall is a simple structure that can have a big impact on an attic conversion. The kneewall is a short framed wall that drops down from the slope of the rafters to the floor, creating a plumb wall surface. This simple structure can change the perception of the space and make it more livable in the process, and it also provides abundant storage opportunities.

The wall itself is easy to construct, requiring only a minimum of experience and tools. The wall described in the following steps makes use of a top plate that has been beveled along one edge to create a flush nailing surface for drywall. However, if ripping a bevel on a long framing member seems a little daunting, you can just as easily use a plain top plate and simply butt the drywall for the vertical surface against the drywall that is installed to face the rafters.

Before you begin framing the wall, you'll need to decide exactly how high you'd like the kneewall to be. Traditionally knee walls have been used to block off the "living" space as defined by code, essentially closing off that part of the attic with unusable headroom. Typically, this meant building a knee wall 5 feet tall. But that's not a hard-and-fast rule.

Many homeowners opt for a 48-inch wall—the exact measurement of a sheet of drywall hung horizontally.

As you design your kneewall, keep in mind that the space you're closing off has potential as storage space—not only in its raw form, but to accommodate built-in shelves or cabinets. If you think you'll need access to the area behind the kneewall, you should construct a simple door out of plywood, with a screwed-on handle, and flush-mount hinges. Just remember to add weather stripping and possibly foam board insulation on the back of the door, to ensure the doorway doesn't become a weak point in the insulated shell of the attic.

Tools & Materials ▸

Hammer	Table saw
Tape measure	2 × 6s, 2 × 4s,
Cordless drill	1 × 2 and 1 × 4
Clamps	hardwood pieces
Wood screws	¼" plywood
Carpenter's pencil	Wood glue
Circular saw	

In most attic conversions, kneewalls are necessary to maximize usable floor space and meet building codes. Typically 4 to 5 ft. high, a kneewall is a perfect location for recessed storage shelves or drawers that extend back into the unused area on the other side of the wall.

How to Frame a Kneewall

Cut a straight 2 × 4 a few inches longer than the planned kneewall height and then position it against a rafter, making sure it is plumb. Trace the rafter edge onto the top of the 2 × 4 (inset) to identify the required cutting angle for the tops of the new wall studs.

Snap a chalkline across all the rafter bottoms to mark the top plate placement. Do the same along the subfloor for the bottom plate, using a plumb bob to make sure the bottom plate is directly beneath the top plate.

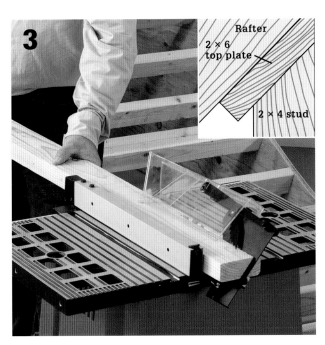

Bevel the front edge of the 2 × 4 or 2 × 6 top plate to make a flush nailing surface for hanging the drywall. Nail the top and sole plates along chalk lines and mark stud positions on both.

Cut and install the wall studs to fit between the top and bottom plates at 16" on-center spacing. Make the top cuts at the angle from Step 1. Check each stud to make sure it is plumb, and attach it by toenailing to the plates with 10d common nails. Install insulation and wallcoverings. If you will be installing wiring in the wall, it is easier to run cable and install boxes before the wallcoverings are attached.

Recessed Kneewall Storage

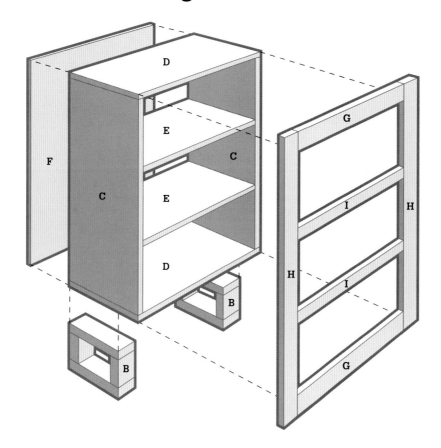

Cutting List ▶

KEY	PART	MATERIAL	PIECES	SIZE
A	Header and sill	2 × 4s	1 each	30½"
B	Pedestals	2 × 4s	2	14 × 15"
C	Sides	¾" plywood	2	19 × 28½"
D	Top and bottom	¾" plywood	2	19 × 30"
E	Shelves	¾" plywood	2	19 × 28½"
F	Back panel	¼" plywood	1	30 × 30"
G	Rails	1 × 4	2	28½"
H	Stiles	1 × 4	2	35½"
I	Shelf rails	1 × 2	2	28½"

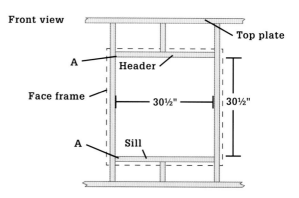

Front view

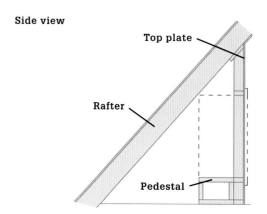

Side view

How to Create Recessed Kneewall Storage

Frame the rough opening in the kneewall. The rough opening should be ⅛" greater on all sides than the dimensions of the storage cabinet you'll be recessing. Attach the 2 × 4 header and sill to studs at the side of the opening. Add cripple studs, centered side to side, below the sill and above the header.

Install 2 × 4 support frames behind the wall. The tops of the frames should be flush with the top of the sill. Make sure the frames are level and securely fastened to the attic floor.

Cut the cabinet parts and the shelf stock from high-quality ¾" plywood. Draw layout lines for shelves on the side panels.

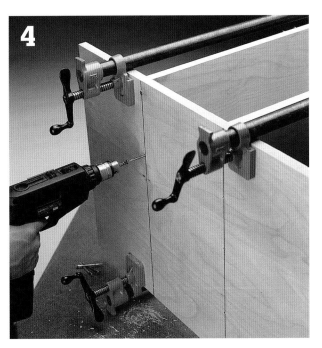

Attach the shelves to the side panels with countersunk 2½" wood screws driven through pilot holes in the cabinet sides and into the shelf edges. Clamp and square all parts before driving fasteners.

(continued)

5

Fasten the top and bottom cabinet panels to the edges of the side panels with countersunk wood screws. Reinforce the joints with glue and make sure the parts are all square before driving the screws.

6

Screw the ¼" plywood back panel to the case with 1¼" screws spaced every 10" or so. Be sure that the back is lined up exactly square to the cabinet.

Outer Face Frame ▸

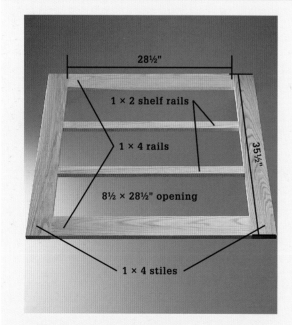

28½"

1 × 2 shelf rails

1 × 4 rails

35½"

8½ × 28½" opening

1 × 4 stiles

Build the outer face frame with clear 1 × 4 hard- or softwood. The outer frame will cover the rough edges of the wall opening. The shelf rails are made from 1 × 2 hardwood.

7

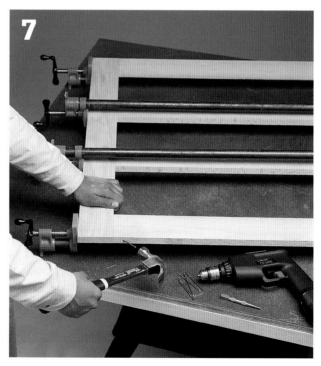

Make the face frame from hardwood lumber. You can glue, clamp, and nail the joints with finish nails, or use a cabinetmaking technique such as plate joinery (biscuit joints) or pocket screws. If nailing, be sure to drill precisely located pilot holes for the finish nails.

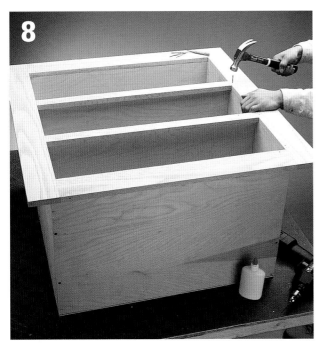

8

Attach the face frame to front edges of the storage cabinet. Glue the frame and then predrill and nail it to the case with finish nails. Use a nailset to sink the nails.

9

Set the shelf unit in place and check for level and plumb. Shim as necessary and nail face frame to header, sill, and side studs with finish nails. Sink the nails, putty over all nail heads, sand, and paint or finish.

Option: Add Drawers

Fasten drawer slide hardware to the tops of the shelves according to the hardware manufacturer's instructions. You can use side-mount hardware, but for lighter duty the center-mount slides that attach underneath the drawers are easier to work with.

Install drawers. If you have some basic carpentry skills, making your own overlay-type drawers is not difficult. You can also have them made to size at any cabinetmaking shop.

Attic Addition Ceilings

The dramatic shapes and angles formed by rafters create many possibilities for finishing an attic ceiling. The simplest solution is just to hang drywall running to the peak of the ceiling, an attractive option that creates appealing visual space with a basic ceiling surface. But there are other options that might better suit your own attic conversion, tastes, and style.

For instance, you may want the more conventional look of a horizontal ceiling. If the roof ventilation system includes gable-end vents, you'll need to box in a space to ensure free flow of air from the top of the rafter cavities to the gable end vents. A horizontal ceiling is the solution. It will also be the option of choice in attics where collar ties—braces between opposing rafters—have been used. Dealing with collar ties can be a challenge, and it's worth speaking with a structural engineer to determine if they can be removed or moved further up if they intrude into the usable headroom of the space. If you do hang a horizontal ceiling surface in the space to cover up the collar ties, check the building code to see if the ties are large enough to carry the weight. Ultimately, though, you may just find a flat ceiling more appealing because it establishes a continuity with the other rooms in the house.

Exceptionally detailed craftsmanship defines this dramatic tongue-in-groove ceiling. The wood boards are complemented by trim that terminates in an artistic overhead light.

The flat ceiling in this attic suite flattens the sharp angle of the walls and allows for ceiling fixtures to be wired into the space.

If a flat ceiling is a bit too mundane for your tastes, consider a paneled ceiling. Tongue-and-groove paneling is often used on cathedral ceilings, and the combination of warm wood and soaring angles never fails to attract the eye. You can choose from a wide variety of woods. Pine is the most common and often the least expensive. Choose a stain or finish that will complement the rest of the space. You'll also select from different board thicknesses, although most building codes mandate that thin boards be backed with Type X drywall as a fire stop. Otherwise, you'll install the boards right over the rafters.

Part of the beauty of tongue-in-groove ceilings is that the boards are "blind-nailed"—nailed through the tongue that is subsequently hidden in the groove of the board next to it. So no nailheads mar the surface appearance. Cut the boards with a compound miter saw, which can handle the complex cuts in attics with multiple angles created by hip roofs or dormers.

Installing a tongue-in-groove board ceiling is a demanding undertaking. You'll need to accurately estimate the material you need—based on the "reveal" measurement only—and add 10 to 15 percent more for waste. The boards must be stained or finished before installation—otherwise you'll see unfinished edges in the tongue and groove as the wood shrinks and expands. But with attention to detail and by working slowly, you can have an impressive ceiling that will add immeasurably to your finished attic.

How to Frame a Flat Attic Ceiling

Mark a storyboard for the height of the ceiling. Start at one end of the attic and mark the bottom edge of a rafter while holding the storyboard plumb against it, with the height mark aligned with the rafter edge. Do the same at the other end, and snap a chalk line between the two marks.

Select a perfectly straight board to use as a straightedge, then hold it with a level, from the mark on the beginning rafter across to the facing rafter. Mark the rafter with ceiling height line. Repeat at the other end of the attic and again snap a chalk line between the two marks.

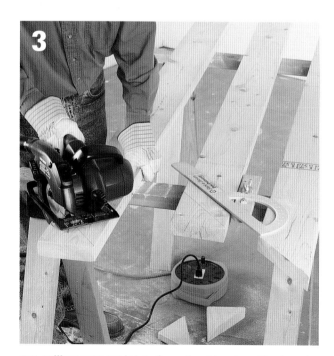

Cut ceiling support joists from 2 × 6 lumber. Check each joist for the crown edge, and cut the ends on an angle to match the roof slope, so that the crown edge of each joist will face up when the joist is nailed into place. Cut joists about ½" short to prevent them from touching roof sheathing.

Nail each joist in place, with three nails on each end. Double check level after nailing the first side, and begin installing ceiling drywall once all joists are in place.

How to Install a Tongue-and-Groove Ceiling

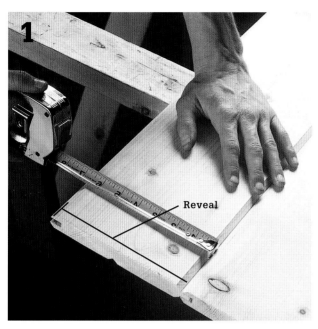

Plan the board layout by measuring the reveal (the width of the board without the tongue) of two boards attached together. Calculate the number of boards you'll need to cover one side of the ceiling by dividing the reveal depth into the space between the bottom of the wall and the peak (you'll be cutting the bottom board to adjust).

Mark the top of the first row of boards on the rafters at both ends of the ceiling by measuring down from the peak the distance in your calculations from step 1. Snap a chalk line across the rafters for the placement of the first row. You may need to adjust the width of the first row of boards so that you don't end up with a thin strip at the top.

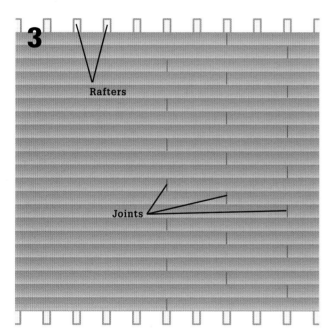

Where boards aren't long enough to run completely across the ceiling, you'll need to have joints. Stagger the joints in a three-part bond pattern as shown here (or randomly), which will minimize their visual impact. Ensure that each joint falls on top of the middle of a rafter. Select boards as close to the same coloring and grain as possible for each row.

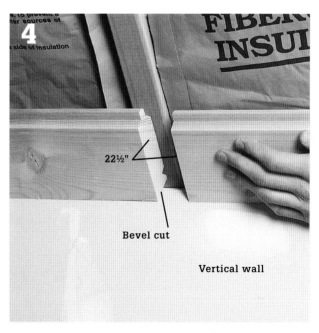

Prepare the starter row. Make a bevel cut to remove the grooved bottom edge, with the bevel angled so the board fits flush against the wall. You can use a table saw or a circular saw and straightedge guide to make the bevel cuts. If the starter row will have end joints, cut the board ends at 22½° so they form a scarf joint.

(continued)

5

Nail the starter board in place, with the beveled side flush against the wall and the edge of the tongue aligned along the chalk line. Nail the wall side first, about 1" from the edge into each rafter. Blind-nail through the tongue, angling the nail 45° downwards. Leave ⅛" between the end of the board and the end wall to allow for expansion.

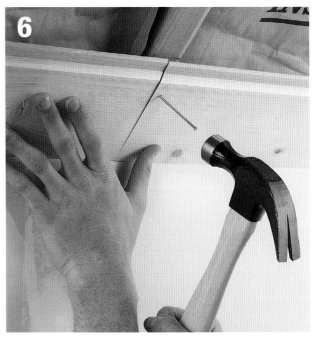

6

Cut and nail up remaining boards in the starter row, fitting the scarf joints snugly together. Predrill nail holes at an angle through the face of the top board at the scarf joint, so that the drill penetrates the bottom board scarf cut. Nail the boards together and use a nailset to sink all the face nails in the first row.

7

Cut the first board for the second row to length as necessary, and then slide the groove over the tongue of the starter row board. Slide a scrap piece of board onto the tongue of the top board, and gently hammer it down into position, securely seating the groove over the tongue. Blind-nail the second row board into place.

8

Continue nailing new rows in place, stopping every other row to measure from the peak to the top of the last row in several points, to check that the rows are parallel. Adjust as necessary by changing how snugly one row's grooves fit into the tongue below it.

9

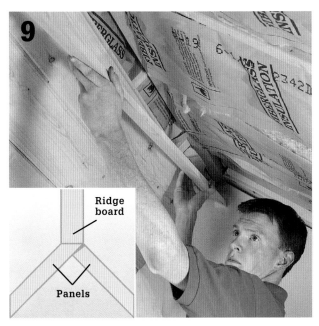

Rip the boards in the last row as necessary so that they fit snugly against the ridge board. Face nail the boards in place as before and install the boards for the opposite side of the ceiling. When you install the final row for that side, cut the boards to form a closed joint directly under the ridge, and sink all nailheads when you're done.

10

Finish the ceiling with molding nailed along joints at walls, chases, and other obstacles, at inside and outside corners, and where design dictates as a decorative element. Bevel the edges of the trim and miter the ends as necessary to fit the ceiling slope and angles.

Solutions for Paneled Ceilings

Collar ties can be left as is when a ceiling is paneled around them, but they create an unfinished look. To add visual interest to the ceiling, clad the collar ties with cut panels. Finish the ceiling and then rip the same stock as you used on the ceiling to the width of the collar ties (sides and bottom). Miter the ends to fit snugly against the ceiling and nail the boards in place.

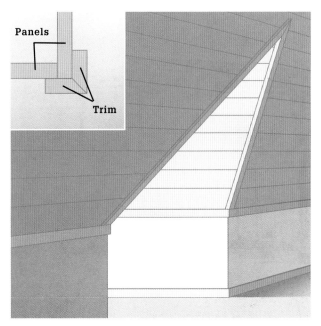

Mitered trim can add a dynamic, polished appearance to any tongue-in-groove ceiling. This type of trim is especially useful on challenging angled outside corners, such as the joints between a dormer's interior surfaces and the sloped ceiling of the finished space. Hide the butt joints at these edges with miter cut trim as shown in the detail.

Other Additions & Conversions

Complete room additions and smaller bumpouts are great ways to increase the livable space in your home, but they are far from the only ways. You can also convert unused or extra space rather than build new.

Basements can be wonderful locations for certain types of rooms. The quiet of the space is ideal for a bedroom, and the large footprint of a basement makes it a wonderful candidate for a family room. All you need to start with is a basement that is dry, and has enough head room to satisfy codes for living spaces.

If your basement doesn't fit the bill, your garage may be a better option. Garages—detached or attached—are usually large enough to house just about any room you care to put there. An attached two-car garage can become a master suite, while a detached garage might serve as the perfect guest "cottage" or home office.

You may, however, be less inclined to take on a full-blown conversion or addition, in which case a sunroom may be right for you. Sunrooms are more modest additions, but are still capable of making a big impact. Walls of glass can provide shelter for overwintering plants, or a restful sitting area where you can get your daily dose of vitamin D.

Just as with any other type of addition, the first stop for any of these options is always the local building department to determine what local codes do and don't allow. But once you've got the legal green light, you can let your imagination lead you to design and convert an ideal space for you and your family.

In this chapter:

- Garage Conversions
- Basement Remodeling Codes & Practices
- Basement Conversions
- Sunrooms

Garage Conversions

Garages are generally not the first place you'd look to expand your home's living space. If they're not actively housing a car or two, they are usually packed with all those odds and ends that don't seem to fit anywhere else in the house. Between a lack of light and a wealth of clutter, it can be hard to see the potential in a garage. But the garages might be the ideal space for the home addition you have in mind. The basic structure is already framed and in place, with a roof, walls, and even a door or two (one of them probably needs some downsizing). The framing is usually left exposed, making it easy to run utilities through the walls. Most garages are already wired for electrical service and, in some cases, plumbing. All this means that the work and expense of a garage conversion can be significantly less than that of a room addition built from scratch, with the same result. The only real problem is finding another place to park your car.

The footprint of a typical garage makes for very usable space. It's usually big enough for any type of room you want, from a well-equipped home theater to a large home office. And the shape of the average two-car garage lends itself to being neatly divided in a number of different ways. This makes the garage a candidate for a small suite, like a new master bedroom with a spa bathroom.

A garage conversion can take many forms and uses. The "man lair" is one, and the mother-in-law apartment is another (these two uses seldom co-exist).

The type of addition you convert your garage to will be partially influenced by whether the garage is attached or detached. Some rooms, such as a bedroom or a pantry and work area for a kitchen are better suited for an attached garage, where they can be integrated into the existing floorplan. A detached garage, on the other hand, is ideal for rooms such as home offices and rec rooms for teenagers, where noise and visitors to the space can be isolated from the house. But whatever type of room you want to build, a garage conversion begins with a thorough cleaning of the garage and assessment of the existing structure. Only when you have a good idea of the raw space you have to work with will you know with certainty what should go there.

Planning a Garage Conversion

The first step in converting a garage to a living space is to determine if local codes even allow it. Municipalities seeking to preserve the nature of the community often prohibit garage conversions to prevent single-family dwellings from becoming multi-unit structures. Even where it's allowed, codes likely insist that a garage space be updated to the standards governing living spaces. For example, the minimum requirements for the roof structure over a detached garage are substantially more modest than the requirements for the roof over a living area. And you may need to beef up the footings.

Once you're satisfied that code requirements won't prove a hindrance, assess the condition of your garage:

- **Look for obvious issues** that might create a problem in converting the structure, such as water damage or insect infestation.
- **Determine what level** of electrical and plumbing service, if any, your garage currently receives.
- **Inspect the floor.** Aside from fixing cracks or other damage, you'll probably want to plan for a new subfloor and insulation. Keep in mind that garage floors are either canted toward a central drain, or sloped toward the door. Depending on the situation and available headroom, you may want to build an elevated floor framed from 2 × 4s using the same principles as building a floor for a room addition.

Attached or Detached? ▶

Detached or attached garages present different challenges. It will be easier to run HVAC services to an attached garage, but structural changes—such as moving or enlarging the door from the house to the garage—need to be carefully weighed against the possible impact they will have on the rest of the home's structure. A detached garage will need greater insulation and may need brand new services run to the structure. HVAC solutions for the detached garage will most likely be local, such as baseboard heating and window air conditioners.

A house with an attached garage

A large detached garage

Garage Conversion Issues

Regardless of what type of garage you are converting, consult an architect or builder to help you develop your expansion plans. Although the structural work needed to convert the garage will be modest in comparison to a full-room addition, you'll still need work permits, a set of plans, and a precise idea of what kinds of changes you want to make.

Other issues will figure into your planning as well. A below-grade garage may have one or more walls of concrete block or poured concrete. This may entail installing furring strips or framing a stud wall along the concrete wall so that insulation, a vapor barrier, and drywall can be installed. The driveway also presents a challenge. Left as is, it will be a visual oddity, terminating at what will be a finished wall. Excavating it is a large undertaking but there are other solutions. For instance, you can cover the driveway with raised garden beds (terraced if the driveway is on a slope) to create an extension of your landscaping. If the garage is large enough, you may prefer to keep a modest workshop by leaving the garage door intact and beginning the addition with a wall placed 6 to 8 feet behind it. This leaves enough room for a workbench and tools.

Clutter is present in just about any garage and is relatively easy to deal with. Of greater concern, if you're thinking of converting your garage, is a block or concrete exterior wall, especially if the exterior side is partially below grade. The mechanic's bays covered in wood are not particularly problematic since you'll almost certainly be reinforcing the concrete floor or making other alterations to it.

You'll also need to figure out where your car will go once the conversion is complete (check local laws—some prohibit on-street parking after dark), and what you will do with the tools, equipment, and various other materials currently being stored in the garage. If your garage is full, you may even want to plan the construction of a utility shed—or possibly a carport—as part of the garage conversion project. Finally, you'll want to include in your planning the details that ensure the addition blends with the existing structure: matching siding, window and door casing, window sizes and styles, and architectural elements.

Some garages already have features that you can include in your conversion design. An arched picture window can easily be worked into the plan, and if it has an existing electrical subpanel with at least 50 amps of service you've got a good start.

What about the driveway? In most cases, if you're adding living space in an attached garage, you're probably compensating for the lost parking space with a detached garage. The driveway, naturally, should go with it. The existing driveway likely will be broken up and replaced with a lawn or garden feature.

Basement Conversions

What do you want your basement to look like? Is there a missing room in your house that you've always dreamed about having? A basement bar? A family room? A guest bedroom? A wine cellar? Perhaps a home theater or a state-of the-art workshop? As long as you do the required work to make the basement space safe and comfortable, there is virtually no limit to the number of finishing possibilities. The most popular basement rooms are a family/rec room and a bedroom. With each of these, a basement bathroom is a good fit—even if it is a small half-bath.

Family rooms: Parents love basement family rooms for many reasons, chief among them that they segregate the mess and noise that tends to follow kids. If your basement has a walkout level (a very common setup), you can create an easy transition between indoor and outdoor play areas with a simple patio door. If you enjoy having friends over for backyard cookouts or to watch a ball game, a basement rec room is a perfect place, and it can usually be located with easy access to the grill. Basements tend to stay cool in the summer, which makes the family room a great place for kids to hang out on summer break. But add a gas fireplace and you can make the room a cozy gathering place in winter as well.

Bedrooms: A basement bedroom is a dream come true for many kids, especially as they enter their teens.

It offers enough distance from mom and dad yet is close enough that kids still feel secure. And if the bedroom happens to be located next to a family room with a big screen TV and full video hookups, your basement will quickly become sleepover central. A basement bedroom is also a great location for a guest bedroom, perhaps even one that does double duty as a craft room or home office.

Other rooms: Some rooms are naturally at home in a basement. This is especially true for rooms that support noisy or messy activities: a workshop, a home theater, a laundry room, or an art studio. Some rooms benefit from the relative coolness of a basement. Among them are wine cellars (with tasting tables of course), pantries, and general storage space. If you or someone in your family enjoys an activity that is high impact, finding a spot for it in the basement is a good solution for everyone. A basement gym, a practice room for the band, a dance studio, or even a metal shop all fit better in a basement environment than in other areas of your house.

Dream rooms: Basements, especially in newer homes, offer large spaces that can be claimed for big rooms. A dream spa and bath with a jetted tub and sauna; a billiards lounge, where you actually have enough room to make unobstructed shots; a home for your model railroad; a hot tub party room—the options are virtually endless.

A full kitchen in the basement is a bit unusual, but if you've always dreamt of being able to work in an Olympic-sized kitchen, you may find that an unfinished basement is the best spot to find the floor space you need. A state-of-the-art ventilation system is a crucial element if you install a kitchen underground. And unless you're intending to add a basement dining room, be sure to allocate some of the floor space for a dining table or a banquette.

A basement room doesn't have to be a room at all. Here, a quiet corner beneath a staircase is finished out to create an intimate reading and conversation spot. More of a stopping off point than a room, it nevertheless adds a new dimension to the living space in this home. It also makes use of a lovely window that's tucked in above the knee wall foundation.

A finished basement can be a single room or a whole series of rooms, as is the case with the living suite seen here. By applying the same decorative elements throughout the suite, the homeowners were able to reinforce the overall design and create a feeling of openness that carries from room to room.

A sunken feeling is a natural effect of a basement room, as in this sitting room that is very reminiscent of a 1970s-era sunken living room. Warm neutral colors and an inviting fireplace successfully fight back against the coldness that can consume a basement.

Let your imagination run wild in your basement. Your design sensibilities may be constrained by convention in the more formal areas of your house, but when you're decorating your remodeled basement, you can reach deep into your bag of design tricks and pull in the colors and styles that let you express yourself fully.

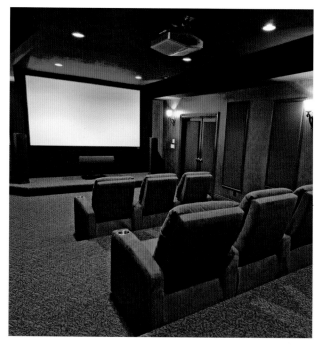

Simple as 1-2-3: excellent lighting, great acoustics, and super-comfortable seating add up to a home theater that packs 'em in every night.

A basement bathroom is a real convenience if you're adding lower level living space, such as a bedroom or family room. If you have the space and the resources to install a three-quarter bath or a full bath, you'll appreciate the added functionality.

Guest bedrooms are one of the most common basement remodeling projects. Often, they are designed as multipurpose rooms so you can use the room as a home office when it is not being employed as a bedroom.

A family room is a great addition to a basement because it keeps the rumpus, clutter, and noise on its own level. A gas fireplace adds warmth to the room.

An intimate wine cellar fits perfectly in a basement. (The presence of the word *cellar* in the name is a good clue.) You'll want to wall off the area and appoint it with racking systems and in some cases climate control. A tasting table makes the room suitable for entertaining.

Basement Remodeling Codes & Practices

Converting a basement into livable space involves conquering a set of challenges that are unique to subterranean construction. Basement remodeling and finishing is regulated with the same codes and practices that apply to any living space. In addition, your construction must deal with the constant threat posed by water runoff and moisture that percolates in through the adjoining soil. Air quality in a cool environment with high relative humidity that favors mold growth is also a concern. Egress (the ability to get in and out easily) is very important in basements—you must have an additional door or egress-size window in case the main entryway is blocked. Even gravity can work against you in a basement, where draining waste water may require a pump to be ejected efficiently.

Building codes distinguish between habitable space and nonliving space. All habitable rooms must have a footprint of at least seventy square feet with at least one wall that's seven feet or longer. The exception is a kitchen, which can be as small as fifty square feet in some instances. However, it should be noted that a small bedroom is usually considered to be in the one hundred square foot to one hundred fifty square foot range, so you should consider a seventy square foot bedroom only under extremely tight conditions. Minimum ceiling height is seven and a half feet, with some exceptions (see illustration, this page). Beams or ductwork may not drop down more than six inches from the ceiling.

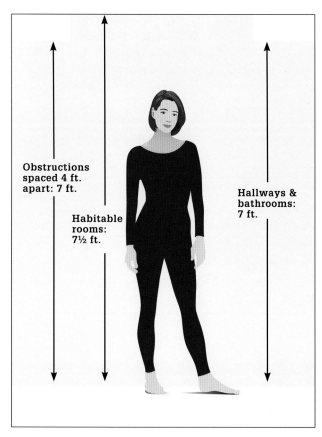

Basement headroom is often limited by beams, ducts, pipes, and other elements. Typical minimums for ceiling height are shown here: 7½ ft. for habitable rooms; 7 ft. for bathrooms and hallways; 7 ft. for obstructions spaced no less than 4 ft. apart.

Additional Requirements for Building in Basements ▸

Permanently installed appliances, such as furnaces and water heaters, must be fully accessible for inspection, service, repair, and replacement. A dedicated furnace room must have a door at least 20" wide and large enough for passage of the furnace. There should be a minimum 30"-wide area of clear space for maintenance access. Check with your local building department for combustion air supply requirements.

Clothes dryers must exhaust to the exterior.

Bathrooms without natural ventilation must have artificial ventilation of at least 50 cu ft. per minute that is vented to the exterior. Ventilation in half baths (no tub or shower) can exhaust into the attic in some areas.

Electrical service panels may not be located in bathrooms or in closets.

GFCI receptacles or circuits are required in bathrooms, unfinished spaces, and on countertops within 6 ft. of a faucet.

Receptacles are required every 6 ft. in all habitable rooms. They are also required in any wall area wider than 2 ft., laundry areas, and in any hallway longer than 10 ft.

A habitable room, storage room, utility room, hallway, or staircase must have at least one switch-operated light fixture. Habitable rooms must also have an amount of window glass area equal to at least 8% of the area of the floor. At least half of the window area must be openable for unobstructed ventilation. Artificial lights and mechanical ventilation may be substituted under some conditions.

Unfinished areas must have windows with an unobstructed ventilation area equal to 1% of the floor area.

Egress Window Considerations

If your home has an unfinished or partially finished basement, it's an enticing and sensible place to expand your practical living space. Another bedroom or two, a game room, or maybe a spacious home office are all possibilities. However, unless your basement has a walk-out doorway, you'll need to add an egress window to make your new living space meet building codes. That's because the International Residential Code (IRC) requires two forms of escape for every living space—an exit door and a window large enough for you to climb out of, or for an emergency responder to enter.

Code mandates that a below-ground egress window will have a minimum opening area of at least 5.7 square feet. There are stipulations about how this open area can be proportioned: The window must be at least 20 inches wide and 24 inches high when open. Additionally, the installed window's sill height must be within 44 inches of the basement floor to permit easy escape. Typical basement windows do not meet these requirements. A large egress window also requires an oversized window well. The well must be at least 36 inches wide and project 36 inches or more from the foundation. If the window well is deeper than 44 inches, it must have a fixed ladder for escape.

What does this all mean for the ambitious do-it-yourselfer? The good news is that if you've got the nerve to cut an oversized opening in your home's foundation, and you don't mind spending some quality time with a shovel, installing a basement egress window is a manageable project. Here's a case where careful planning, a building permit, and some help can save you considerable money over hiring a contractor to do the work.

Contact your local building department to learn more about specific egress requirements that apply to your area.

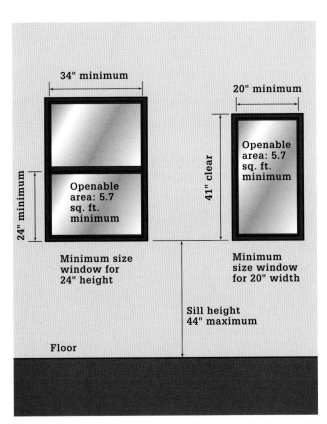

In order to satisfy building codes for egress, a basement window must have a minimum opening of 5.7 sq. ft. through one sash, with at least 20" of clear width and 24" of clear height. Casement, double-hung, and sliding window styles can be used, as long as their dimensions for width and height meet these minimum requirements.

Egress window wells must be at least 36" wide and project 36" from the foundation. Those deeper than 44" must have a means of escape, such as a tiered design that forms steps, or an attached ladder. Drainage at the bottom of the well should extend down to the foundation footing drain, with pea gravel used as the drainage material.

Sunrooms

A typical sunroom project can be a lot like putting on an addition. The new room expands, or bumps out from, the home's original footprint and includes all of the construction elements of an indoor space: a foundation and insulated floor, walls, and roof, plus electrical and heating and cooling systems for all your creature comforts. Also, like an addition, a sunroom can have a big impact on both the interior and exterior architecture of the home, and, if planned properly, can improve the quality and function of nearby rooms.

Because a sunroom is all about enjoying the light and warmth from the sun, deciding where to place the room is a critical consideration. Your choices of location may be limited by several factors, such as lot size and local zoning laws, so it's best to consult your city office at the beginning of the planning process. Another big decision lies in how the sunroom will be built. Most people prefer to hire out the project and either have a manufactured sunroom installed by a professional crew or go the custom route and have the room designed and built from scratch. But if you're handy and up to the job, you might choose to build a sunroom yourself using a complete kit.

It's also possible to create a sunroom without adding on. Given the right location and good sun exposure, an existing room can be turned into a sunroom by installing lots of windows and perhaps a new entry door. And some homeowners find they can save space and money (or satisfy zoning restrictions) by converting a roofed porch or patio or even an elevated deck into a sunroom.

Whatever your dreams for a sun-filled haven, this section introduces you to many of the basic considerations that go into planning and creating a sunroom. As you begin your research, consult with local building professionals and other expert sources for more advice that's specific to your project. Product manufacturers, companies that specialize in sunroom design and construction, and even neighbors who have sunrooms also can be valuable sources for information.

As year-round living space, a sunroom must be designed and built with accommodations for seasonal heating and/or cooling, air circulation, energy efficiency, security, and, of course, plenty of daylight.

Construction Options

There are a handful of different ways you can go about building a new sunroom. The most popular option is to hire out the construction and/or installation to a professional builder or a firm that specializes in sunrooms. Among this group of pros, some specialize in custom projects, some work directly with manufacturers to install modular (prefabricated) sunrooms, and some do both custom and prefab work. Another option is to build the sunroom yourself using a do-it-yourself kit, which can save you a lot of money. However, unless a sunroom kit is made with insulated (double-pane) windows, it's probably not practical for year-round use in cold climates. And finally, if you have the inclination and the wherewithal, you can design and build your own custom sunroom, most likely over the course of many, many weekends.

CUSTOM SUNROOMS

A custom, site-built sunroom addition offers the ultimate in design flexibility. It's also the best way to ensure architectural continuity—that is, building something that looks like part of your original house. If your budget allows, a custom sunroom can include whatever you want, from a creative layout to a soaring cathedral ceiling to any door and window configuration that suits your home.

Custom sunrooms are typically built much like standard room additions, with wood-framed, insulated walls and roof. The exterior wall finish can be the same material as your house siding or it can introduce a different material that complements the facade's decorative scheme. The same goes for all interior finishes. As for the floor, a popular option for sunrooms is to pour a new insulated concrete slab, which can be used as the finish flooring or be covered with other flooring materials. The floor can also be built as a standard wood-frame structure.

If you're in the market for a tailor-made sunroom, talk to several local contractors who specialize in projects similar to yours. Be sure to check out the quality of their work on other projects they've completed around town, and talk to those home-owners about their experiences with the contractors. Depending on the complexity of your plans, you might also want to hire an architect or a qualified designer for help with any or all stages of the design process. Most architects can also be retained to serve as a project manager or to oversee the construction phase of the job.

This shallow, two-story sunroom benefited from custom design and construction to take full advantage of the limited space available and to blend with the European styling of the home.

(continued)

Large yet well proportioned, this sunroom addition bears the marks of custom work in its unique, Asian-inspired details, like the extended roof eave and integrated gutter with rain chains in place of conventional downspouts.

MANUFACTURED SUNROOMS

As their name indicates, manufactured sunrooms (also called modular or prefab) are assembled from factory-made parts that are shipped to your home for quick installation by a trained crew. The advantage of manufactured rooms is that they are typically less expensive than custom creations, and the entire process, from planning to design to job completion, can take as little as a month or two. Prefab sunrooms are generally made with low-maintenance materials like aluminum and vinyl, which makes them both durable and easy to care for. The downsides of this type of sunroom are limited design possibilities and finish options, and somewhat generic styling.

Most sunroom manufacturers operate through local dealers who offer turnkey service. After an in-home consultation with the customer, the dealer puts together a design for the room and offers a quote for the complete package. The final price typically includes all necessary preparation work, like pouring a foundation and a floor, as well as the installation. Product options vary by manufacturer; most offer high-performance windows and glazed roof panels as upgrade items, and some offer wood cladding instead of vinyl for the interior of frame members.

Because you're using the same company for virtually every aspect of the sunroom project, it pays to shop around for the right products and a reputable dealer who offers competitive pricing. Visit previous jobs of each prospective vendor, and talk to other customers about their satisfaction with the installation work and the sunroom products.

Manufactured sunrooms are all about construction efficiency, but it takes an experienced crew to complete the prep work, room assembly, and tie-in to the house.

DIY SUNROOMS

Designed with simple, modular construction, do-it-yourself sunrooms are flat-packed and shipped to your door ready to assemble. The complete kits include roof panels, windows, screens, doors, and any extras that you order from the factory. In addition to the easy installation, one of the best features of this type of sunroom is its light weight. Thanks in part to their single-pane, non-glass panels and windows, sunroom kits are light enough to install right on top of patio slabs and wood decks.

The non-insulated glazing is the main disadvantage of DIY sunrooms, since the rooms can only be used in moderate temperatures. You'll have to thermally isolate the sunroom from the rest of the house with an insulated wall and entry door, though during the cooler months of early spring and late fall you can usually use the room with supplemental heating.

Many DIY sunrooms can be installed on existing patios and decks, but make sure your installation is approved by the local building department, and be sure to have any supporting structure inspected by an engineer or qualified builder.

Conversions

Converting Temperatures

Convert degrees Fahrenheit (F) to degrees Celsius (C) by following this simple formula: Subtract 32 from the Fahrenheit temperature reading. Then, mulitply that number by 5/9. For example, 77°F - 32 = 45. 45 × 5/9 = 25°C.

To convert degrees Celsius to degrees Fahrenheit, multiply the Celsius temperature reading by 9/5. Then, add 32. For example, 25°C × 9/5 = 45. 45 + 32 = 77°F.

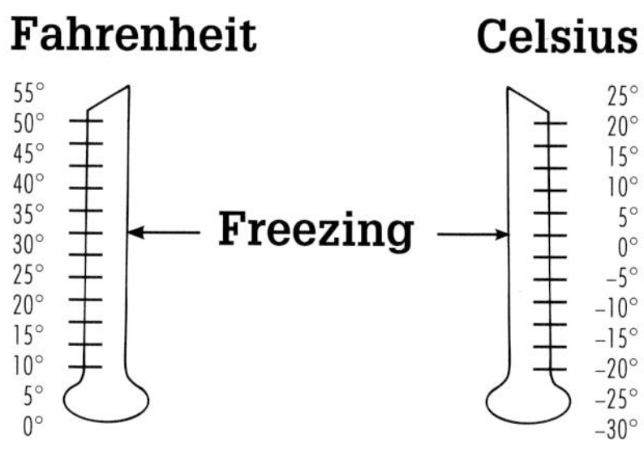

Nails

Nail lengths are identified by numbers from 4 to 60 followed by the letter "d," which stands for "penny." For general framing and repair work, use common or box nails. Common nails are best suited to framing work where strength is important. Box nails are smaller in diameter than common nails, which makes them easier to drive and less likely to split wood. Use box nails for light work and thin materials. Most common and box nails have a cement or vinyl coating that improves their holding power.

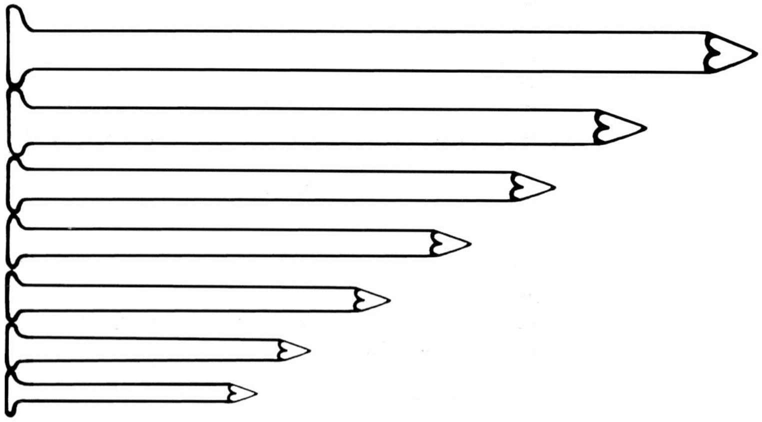

LBS.	MM	IN.
20d	102 mm	4"
16d	89 mm	3½"
10d	76 mm	3"
8d	64 mm	2½"
6d	51 mm	2"
5d	44 mm	1¾"
4d	38 mm	1½"

Metric Plywood Panels

Metric plywood panels are commonly available in two sizes: 1,200 mm × 2,400 mm and 1,220 mm × 2,400 mm, which is roughly equivalent to a 4 × 8-ft. sheet. Standard and Select sheathing panels come in standard thicknesses, while Sanded grade panels are available in special thicknesses.

STANDARD SHEATHING GRADE		SANDED GRADE	
7.5 mm	(5/16 in.)	6 mm	(4/17 in.)
9.5 mm	(3/8 in.)	8 mm	(5/16 in.)
12.5 mm	(1/2 in.)	11 mm	(7/16 in.)
15.5 mm	(5/8 in.)	14 mm	(9/16 in.)
18.5 mm	(3/4 in.)	17 mm	(2/3 in.)
20.5 mm	(13/16 in.)	19 mm	(3/4 in.)
22.5 mm	(7/8 in.)	21 mm	(13/16 in.)
25.5 mm	(1 in.)	24 mm	(15/16 in.)

Resources/Credits

American Institute of Architects
800-AIA-3837
www.aia.org
The Institute supplies a list of local chapters and member architects.

American Society for Testing and Materials (ASTM International)
800-262-1373
www.astm.org
Sets and maintains standards for construction materials and processes worldwide.

APA: The Engineered Wood Association
253-565-6600
www.apawood.org
Supplies a range of information about using engineered wood products in the home.

The Association of Home Appliance Manufacturers (AHAM)
202-872-5955
www.aham.org
Supplies consumers with a range of appliance and safety information, making the site a first stop prior to purchasing appliances for a home addition.

Black & Decker
800-544-6986
www.blackanddecker.com
Supplier of power and hand tools, offering tips and home DIY projects.

Concrete Foundations Association
319-895-6940
www.cfawalls.org
Provides guidance for the consumer considering a concrete foundation, and a listing of certified professionals.

Construction Materials Recycling Association (CMRA)
630-585-7530
www.cdrecycling.org
Promotes the environmentally responsible recycling and reuse of construction materials.

Forest Certification Resource Council
503-224-2205
www.certifiedwood.org
Visitors to their website can access a vast database of certified wood products that are harvested with sustainable forestry practices.

International Code Council
202-783-2348
www.iccsafe.org
Provides code-related information; develops standards and codes widely adopted in communities throughout the US.

National Association of the Remodeling Industry (NARI)
800-611-6274
www.nari.org
Provides information to guide homeowners through remodeling projects, including budget worksheets, a list of licensed remodelers, and more.

National Fenestration Rating Council
301-589-1776
www.nfrc.org
Independent rating organization assessing the energy performance of windows, doors, and skylights. Offers the latest information on energy efficiency in windows and other openings.

National Fire Protection Association
800-344-3555
www.nfpa.org
Publishers of the National Electrical Code. A pdf version is available online.

National Kitchen and Bath Association
800-843-6522
www.nkba.org
A resource for in-depth information on the design and specifications that make kitchens and baths comfortable and enjoyable. Includes a list of certified contractors.

National Roofing Contractor's Association
847-299-9070
www.nrca.net
Provides information and services to help homeowners make informed decisions about replacing and maintaining their roofs.

National Wood Flooring Association
800-422-4556
www.woodfloors.org
Comprehensive information about choosing and buying wood floors, including guidance on finding a qualified flooring professional and sources for different flooring products.

Owens Corning
800-438-7465
www.owenscorning.com
Offers a free homeowner's guide to insulating, installation advice, and other consumer information.

Paint Quality Institute
www.paintquality.com
Supplies painting advice, guidance in choosing paints, and design options.

Underwriter's Laboratory
847-272-8800
www.ul.com
The Underwriter's Laboratory is an independent testing and certification organization, dedicated to supporting the use of safe products in the home.

U.S. Green Building Council
www.usgbc.org
In-depth information about green and sustainable home building practices, including LEED certification.

The Vinyl Siding Institute
888-367-8741
www.vinylsiding.org
Comprehensive information about the latest developments in vinyl siding products.

Photo Credits

Shutterstock, p. 6, 26-27 (all), 28-29 (all), 42, 56-57, 67, 91, 96-97, 100, 101, 166, 174, 177 (top), 190, 195 (right), 201, 223 (left), 224, 225 (bottom);

© **Susan Teare,** p. 8-9, 10-11 (all), 22-23 (all), 24 (both); Architects Michael Minadeo and Partners, Conner and Buck Design Build Contractors, TruexCullins Architecture and Interior Design

Timbercraft Homes, p. 12-13 (all);

© **Jo Ann Snover,** p. 14-15 (all);

Jeannette Architects, p. 16-17 (all);

© **Eric Rosen Architects** (Architecture)/© Erich Koyama (photography), p. 18-19 (all);

Guy Cass Architect, AIA, NCARB, p. 20-21 (all);

© **Mark Samu,** Samu Studios Inc. p. 25 (both);

Distinctive Design, p. 38 (right);

Dominic Mercadante, architect © Brian Vanden Brink, p. 41;

Epoch Homes, p. 102-103 (all);

iStockphoto, p. 170, 228 (bottom right);

© **Andrea Rugg** (for Awad & Koontz Architects Builders, Inc, p. 178), (for Locus Architecture, p. 199 both), (for David Hiede Design, p. 215), 222;

Metalworks, p. 200;

© **Brian Vanden Brink** for Chris Glass, Architect, p. 214;

Clopay, p. 223 (right);

© **Beth Singer**/www.BethSingerPhotographer.com, p. 226, 228 (bottom left);

Elizabeth Whiting & Associates/www.EWAstock.com, p. 227 (top), 228 (top);

Cal Spas, p. 227 (bottom);

Lindal Cedar Homes, p. 232;

Sunporch Structures, Inc., p. 234 (top), 235.

Index